SPIRITUALLY MINDED

An Awareness to Spiritual Warfare

MONTE D. WARE, PHD

WESTBOW
PRESS®
A DIVISION OF THOMAS NELSON
& ZONDERVAN

WestBow Press books may be ordered through booksellers or by contacting:

WestBow Press
A Division of Thomas Nelson & Zondervan
1663 Liberty Drive
Bloomington, IN 47403
www.westbowpress.com
844-714-3454

ISBN: 978-1-6642-1446-0 (sc)
ISBN: 978-1-6642-1447-7 (hc)
ISBN: 978-1-6642-1445-3 (e)

Library of Congress Control Number: 2020923862

Print information available on the last page.

WestBow Press rev. date: 12/17/2020

This book is dedicated to
my wife Denise Ware and all my children,
because of their sacrifices and patiences
through out the years. And last but not
least to Chancellor Vera Milton, who
pushed me and many of my classmates
to achieve a higher level of education.

GOD BLESS YOU ALL

For to be carnally minded is death; but to
be spiritually minded is life and peace.

—Romans 8:6

Contents

Chapter One
SPIRITUAL AWARENESS

Spiritual awareness is simply defined as having the perception and knowledge of an invisible world existing all around you. The spiritual realm is a world that only a well-trained eye can see and observe. Many believers operate in a false sense of sight. Leaders mislead their followers into believing that just because they have repented and given their lives to God, they can now see into the spirit realm and their understanding of spiritual things has been highly elevated.

First, let's examine God's awesome plan for His children.

- God knows what He wants for you. "'For I know the plans I have for you,' declares the Lord, 'plans to prosper you and not to harm you, plans to give you hope and a future'" (Jeremiah 29:11 NIV). God's plan in your life is the supreme plan. His plan trumps yours!

- God's primary plan for His people is for all to prosper. "Beloved, I wish above all things that thou mayest prosper and be in health, even as thy soul prospereth" (3 John 2 KJV).

- For God's plan to come to pass, we must put in the work. "But thou shalt meditate therein day and night, that thou mayest observe to do according to all that is written therein: for then thou shalt make thy way prosperous, and then thou shalt have good success" (Joshua 1:8 KJV).

God desires that His children's desires become the same as His. God simply wants all believers to become like His Son. In Romans 8:29 (KJV), God reminds us, "For whom he did foreknow, he also did predestinate to be conformed to the image of his Son, that he might be the firstborn among many brethren."

We are to stride earnestly for the same mind that was also in Christ Jesus. Philippians 2:5 (KJV) says, "Let this mind be in you, which was also in Christ Jesus."

Once a believer obtains spiritual awareness, the invisible door of Christ is revealed. This means that the spiritual door to the kingdom, which is through Christ Jesus, can now be seen. The doorway home is now visible.

Once the visible door of Christ is revealed, the believer is faced with a life-changing decision. *Will I walk through the door and experience God's freedom, or will I stay where I am, bound up, tied up, and a slave to sin?*

The old saying that you can lead a horse to water but can't make him drink is not only a statement of truth but applies to this very situation with the Lord. Jesus has presented Himself as the doorway to the kingdom of heaven. If you and I do not choose to walk through that door, what benefit can it be for those who say they believe?

Now that we comprehend the doorway that leads to our destiny, we see that Jesus paints a beautiful picture of the door through which we are to enter. Jesus completes His assignment (and a well-done job, I might add) in establishing the doorway for those who would hear the word and desire to pursue eternity in the kingdom of God.

After the completion of His work, Jesus ascended back to heaven, sharing with His disciples the next stage of God's awesome plan for salvation. He says to them that He must go and He will send them another comforter (Holy Spirit) from His Father (John 14:16, 14:26, 15:26, 16:7).

With Jesus being the doorway to the kingdom, we ask, "How do we get to that door?" Naturally, Jesus is gone, but He has sent His Spirit (Comforter) to guide us in all truth, to bring back to our remembrance that which He has shared with us. So spiritually, let's break down the components that make it all whole:

- God's kingdom is the place all believers desire to reside upon their expiration date.
- Jesus is the doorway to that kingdom. He is the way, the truth, and the life. He came to establish a doorway

for all those who would believe; we walk by faith and not by sight (2 Corinthians 5:7).

This kingdom we are sharing must be entered before the believer's time runs out. We must truly understand that it is our responsibility to have the kingdom experience here on earth to ensure our kingdom experience in heaven.

Now after Jesus established the doorway, He left and sent the Holy Ghost (Comforter) as a guide to lead all believers to that doorway that would gain them access to the kingdom.

This is the war we are a part of.

God put it all together and created all things with humans in mind as He created. He created the sun, the moon, the stars, and all the celestials to minister to the earth. God created the earth to minister to humankind, and God created humans to minister to Himself (God). Satan can't do anything about what God created so he tries to do something to what God created. Hence, this is where the *war* begins!

In all that God has created, the human being is the only creature that is fair game. As humans, we are the only prize worth hunting in the world. Free will fuels the human consciousness; our gift of free will sets us apart from the rest of creation. This valuable attribute is used to sway and persuade the soul of a human to live a certain lifestyle.

The war that we as humanity have entered into without any choice of our own is a *spiritual war!*

Before one can go into warfare, one must know that they are in a war. Remember this: the best way to win a war is to make the opposing force believe there is no war. This means the aggressor can move around at will without worrying about detection. This strategy gives him complete mobility to go and do whatever he desires.

It is said that the biggest trick the devil ever played is to trick others into believing he does not exist. Flying under the radar is one of the greatest weapons he has in his arsenal.

Once individuals realize that the issues in the society that they once embraced are no more appealing to their sense of direction, they must then choose to stay in that undesirable society or embrace another. "Wherein in time past ye walked according to the course of this world, according to the prince of the power of the air, the spirit that now worketh in the children of disobedience" (Ephesians 2:2 KJV).

Satan has imposed his life, views, and teachings not only on the world but also on us as believers. This is demonstrated when the Bible says we are born into iniquity shaped in sin. "Behold, I was shapen in iniquity; and in sin did my mother conceive me" (Psalm 51:5 KJV).

Where we fall short as believers and nonbelievers is our inability to see spiritually. This reminds me of the movie *The Matrix,* in which Morpheus offers Neo a choice of pills: a red one or a blue one. One pill would leave things as they are; the other pill would open his mind to see reality.

I believe that there are those in the world who would rather leave things as they are instead of knowing the truth. Hosea 4:6 (KJV) says, "My people are destroyed for lack of knowledge: because thou hast rejected knowledge, I will also reject thee."

Unfortunately no pill is going to give you the insight,

knowledge, or abilities to understand and work in the spiritual realm without putting forth a great effort. "But without faith it is impossible to please him: for he that cometh to God must believe that he is, and that he is a rewarder of them that diligently seek him" (Hebrews 11:6 KJV).

Once faith has been established in the believer's life, it is far from being over; now the hard work begins. Faith is just simply the vehicle we use to get to the desired destination. If I were to travel to another country, I would go *by* plane, train, or ship. Each mode of travel is just a vehicle I would use to get to my desired destination.

In Hebrews 11, you will find the actual vehicle many used to achieve great deeds for the Lord. In Hebrews 11:2 (KJV), we see that the word says "by this," referring to faith in verse 1 that the elders obtained a good report. Also, throughout verses 4–31, you will find many references to faith. All refer to faith as "by faith," saying faith is the vehicle used to obtain a particular destination.

Chapter Two
SPIRITUAL WARFARE

For though we walk in the flesh, we do not war after the flesh: (For the weapons of our warfare are not carnal, but mighty through God to the pulling down of strong holds;) Casting down imaginations, and every high thing that exalteth itself against the knowledge of God, and bringing into captivity every thought to the obedience of Christ.

—2 Corinthians 10:3–5 (KJV)

In order for us to deal with spiritual warfare, we must first understand the powerful influences the spiritual world has over the natural world.

John 4:24 (KJV) says, "God is a Spirit: and they that worship him must worship him in spirit and in truth." "God is Spirit" is a better version than the King James Version's "God is a Spirit." The God of the universe dwells in the invisible realm. This is a declaration of His invisible nature. He is not confined to one location.

God is omnipresent. This is a theological term that refers to God's limitless nature or His capacity to be all over the place at all times. God is not like the man-made idols of ancient civilizations that were limited to one altar or place of worship area. God made Himself known in the Bible as the Lord who is all over the place. God was present as Lord in all creation as it is shown in Psalm 139:7–12 (KJV),

> Whither shall I go from thy spirit? or whither shall I flee from thy presence? If I ascend up into heaven, thou art there: if I make my bed in hell, behold, thou art there. If I take the wings of the morning, and dwell in the uttermost parts of the sea; Even there shall thy hand lead me, and thy right hand shall hold me. If I say, Surely the darkness shall cover me; even the night shall be light about me. Yea, the darkness hideth not from thee; but the night shineth as the day: the darkness and the light are both alike to thee.

There is absolutely no escaping Him. He is present in our deepest thoughts. Even as we are formed in the womb, He knows all the days of our future. As it says in Jeremiah 1:5

(KJV), "Before I formed thee in the belly I knew thee; and before thou camest forth out of the womb I sanctified thee, and I ordained thee a prophet unto the nations."

The worship of God must be done in the manner or way that pleases Him; it must be done in the regiment or design that the Creator of the universe has depicted for it to be done.

There is only one design of worship in which God has put forth for His people to partake in or use in worship to Him, and that can be done only through the One (Jesus), who expresses God's invisible nature, as you will find in John 1:18 (KJV), "No man hath seen God at any time; the only begotten Son, which is in the bosom of the Father, he hath declared him."

God's amazing design of worship uses His Son as the catalyst and the connection back to Himself. John 14:6 (KJV) declares, "Jesus saith unto him, I am the way, the truth, and the life: no man cometh unto the Father, but by me."

Let's explore the role of the Son of God in this amazing plan to connect the spiritual world to the natural world. First, let's break up the Bible into four parts:

1. Genesis–Malachi is "Our History." History is defined as a narrative or chronological record of significant events (Genesis 2:4), or generations. The Hebrew word translated as history literally means "genealogy." This tells us where we come from, how we came to be, who our fathers were, and what they did right and wrong. And most important was what did and did not please God.

2. Matthew–John is "The Message." The message is the kingdom. Please understand that Jesus did not come preaching or teaching about Himself. He came preaching and teaching the kingdom of heaven! John the Baptist first proclaimed it in Matthew 3:1–2 and then Jesus Himself in Matthew 4:17. Jesus was modestly powerful. In His reference to Himself, He ensured us that He was the doorway to the kingdom (John 10:1–9).

3. Acts–Jude is "The Conduct." There is a way we are to live in the kingdom. Acts to Jude displays what will and will not be tolerated in the kingdom. After the death, burial, and resurrection of Christ Jesus, things changed, and a whole new covenant was in play. We couldn't live through some of the old ways of doing things that Jesus has now fulfilled (Galatians 6:5; Philippians 3:18; 1 Timothy 3:15).

4. Revelations is "Foresight and Prophecy," that is, our future, what we can expect to come, man's destiny according to man's actions and conduct.

The World's Influences

The New Testament tells of two kingdoms: the kingdom of this world and the kingdom of God.

- The kingdom of this world is under Satan's influence (Luke 4:5–6; John 14:30–31; 1 John 5:18–20; 2 Corinthians 4:3–4). The dominant values of the world include wealth, power, pleasure, revenge, fame, vanity, and status. These things are most important to people who perceive no power or purpose beyond themselves. Worldly values promote jealousies, resentments, and conflicts among people in accordance with Satan's purposes (John 8:44; Acts 5:3; Romans 16:17–20; 2 Corinthians 4:4; Ephesians 2:1–3, 4:25–32; 2 Timothy 2:22–26; 1 John 3:8–10).

- The kingdom of God (also known as the kingdom of heaven) is not a geographic location. It exists within the world among those people who put their faith, trust, and loyalty in God (Luke 17:20–21). The values of the kingdom of God are often the opposite of worldly values. They consist of kindness and respect for all people. Power humility instead of status, fame, and vanity; honesty and generosity instead of wealth; self-control instead of pleasure; forgiveness instead of revenge. Christian values promote peace and goodwill among people in accordance with God's purposes.

These are the things we strive for if we are sincere followers of Christ. We will never achieve perfection in this life, but those who strive to obey God often find a sense of joy and peace that no worldly rewards can match!

Worship Only God

One day, a religious leader asked Jesus which of the commandments was most important.

"The most important one" answered Jesus, "is this: 'Hear, O Israel, the Lord our God, the Lord is one. Love the Lord your God with all your heart and with all your soul and with all your mind and with all your strength.'" (Mark 12:28–30 NIV)

The Hebrews of Old Testament times tended to lapse into worship of pagan deities and statues of animals or other objects, but anything that takes the place of our devotion to God becomes an idol or false god, and the first of the Ten Commandments (Exodus 20:1–6) forbids that. Jesus particularly singled out the love of wealth as a false god (Matthew 6:24; Luke 16:13), and other Bible passages mention greed, covetousness, arrogance, gluttony, and pride as being equivalent to idolatry.

In today's world, many things compete against God for our devotion. These are some of the things that can become modern-day idolatry if we let them become too important to us: excessive attention to material things such as houses, cars, clothes, jewellery, physical appearance, entertainment, and so forth; the pursuit of wealth, power, fame, pleasure, or status; and excessive devotion to self, job, hobbies, country, ideologies, heroes, leaders, and even family.

Biblical References
1 Samuel 15:23; Matthew 6:31–34, 22:34–40; Mark 12:28–31; Luke 10:25–28; Acts 14:11–15; 1 Corinthians 10:14; Galatians 5:19–21; Ephesians 5:5; Colossians 3:5; Philippians 3:18–19; 1 Timothy 6:6–11; 6:17–20; 2 Timothy 3:1–5; Hebrews 13:5; 1 Peter 4:1–6

Respect All People

"The second is this: 'Love your neighbor as yourself.' There is no commandment greater than these" (Mark 12:31 NIV). After saying "Love the Lord your God" is the most important of the commandments, Jesus continued.

The English word *love* has many different meanings, but the Greek word *agape* used in the New Testament is commonly known as "Christian love." It means respect, affection, benevolence, goodwill, and concern for the welfare of the one loved.

In His parable of the good samaritan, Jesus made the point that we should extend our Christian love to all people of the world, regardless of race, religion, nationality, or any other artificial distinction. We must practice that Christian love even toward our enemies (Matthew 5:43–48).

Jesus's golden rule is "Do unto others as you would have them do unto you." We should not say or do anything unless we can answer yes to the question, "Would I want that said or done to me?"

Neither should we fail to do the good things we would expect of others. Love is a widely used and abused word in our English language. We use this word as an everyday throw-away word. We use this word to achieve our ulterior goal, and we misuse it, I do believe, because we don't truly know its value or meaning.

Love is simple to explain. Love means you want the best for the one you say you love. Ironically this is tested when you are not the best thing for the one you say you love. Your job then is to let them go so they can pursue what is best for them.

Biblical References
Leviticus 19:18; Matthew 7:12; Matthew 22:34–40; Mark 12:28–31; Luke 6:31, 10:25–28; John 13:34–35; Romans 13:8–10, 15:1–2; James 2:8

Be Humble

Humility or being humble is a quality of being courteously respectful of others. It is the opposite of aggressiveness, arrogance, boastfulness, and vanity. Acting with humility does not in any way deny our own self-worth. Rather it affirms the inherent worth of all persons. Humility is exactly what is needed to live in peace and harmony with all persons. It dissipates anger and heals old wounds. It allows us to see the dignity and worth of all God's people. Humility distinguishes the wise leader from the arrogant power-seeker (Proverbs 17:7; Matthew 20:20–28).

Biblical References
Matthew 5:5–9, 20:25–28; Mark 9:35; 1 Corinthians 10:24; Ephesians 4:1–6; Philippians 2:2–8; 2 Timothy 2:22–25

Be Honest

Honesty and integrity are held as very important values throughout the Bible, and the Ten Commandments, along with other Bible passages, prohibits any deception to gain an advantage or harm another (Exodus 20:16). Deception may be by false statements, half-truths, innuendo, or a failure to tell the whole truth. It is all too common in advertising, business dealings, politics, and everyday life. We must strongly resist the temptation to engage in any form of theft, cheating, deception, innuendo, slander, or gossip.

Rationalization is a form of self-deception by which we convince ourselves that sinful actions are justified in order to achieve a good result, but this is really just another form of dishonesty (Galatians 6:7–8; James 1:26; 1 John 1:8). Holiness is in living by the commandments, not in achieving an end result (Matthew 4:8–10, 16:26). In biblical teaching, the ends do not justify the means!

Biblical References
Exodus 20:15; Leviticus 19:35–36; Deuteronomy 16:19–20, 25:13–16; Psalm 15:1–5, 24:3–5; Proverbs 10:9, 11:1,3, 12:22, 16:28, 19:1, 20:10, 24:28, 28:6,20; Isaiah 33:15–16; Zechariah 7:9; Mark 10:19; Luke 3:12–14, 16:10–12; 2 Corinthians 4:1–2, 7:2, 8:21; Ephesians 4:25; Philippians 4:8–9; Colossians 3:9; Hebrews 13:18; 1 Peter 2:12, 3:10

Live a Moral Life

"Do you not know that your body is a temple of the Holy Spirit, who is in you, whom you have received from God? You are not your own; you were bought at a price. Therefore honor God with your body" (1 Corinthians 6:19–20 NIV).

Jesus gave a list of actions that constitute immoral uses of the body: evil thoughts, murder, adultery, sexual immorality, theft, false testimony, slander, greed, malice, deceit, lewdness, envy, arrogance, and foolishness. The apostle Paul gave similar lists.

We often think of morality in terms of sexual sins, but according to Jesus, sins such as slander, greed, deceit, and arrogance are equally immoral.

Biblical References
Exodus 20:1–17; Matthew 5:27–28, 15:18–19; Mark 7:20–22, 10:11–12; Romans 13:11–14; 1 Corinthians 6:9–11; Galatians 5:16–26; Ephesians 5:1–7; Colossians 3:5–10; 1 Thessalonians 4:3–9

Be Generous with Time and Money

The Bible tells us to share generously with those in need and says that good things will come to us in turn. Each of us has something to offer to someone in need. We can give our money and time to charity, be a friend to someone who is sick or lonely, do volunteer work, or choose a service-oriented occupation. We may give unselfishly of our time to our spouse, children, or parents.

Biblical References
Leviticus 19:9–10, 25:35–38; Deuteronomy 15:7–11; Proverbs 14:21, 28:27; Isaiah 58:10–11; Matthew 5:42, 6:1–2, 25:31–46; Luke 6:38, 12:33, 21:1–4; Acts 20:35; Romans 12:6–8;

2 Corinthians 9:5–7; Hebrews 13:1–3, 15–16; 1 Timothy 6:17–19; 1 John 3:17

Practice What You Preach; Don't Be a Hypocrite

If there were any groups of people that Jesus couldn't stand, it was hypocrites! The Pharisees of Jesus's times were a religious and political party that insisted on very strict observance of biblical laws on tithing, ritual purity, and other matters. At the same time, many of the Pharisees forgot the true spirit and intent of the law and became self-indulgent, self-righteous, snobbish, and greedy. That led Jesus to remarks such as,

> "Woe to you, teachers of the law and Pharisees, you hypocrites! You are like whitewashed tombs, which look beautiful on the outside but on the inside are full of dead men's bones and everything unclean. In the same way, on the outside you appear to people as righteous but on the inside you are full of hypocrisy and wickedness." (Matthew 23:27–28 NIV)

It is not the things we say that really matter; it is the things we do (Matthew 7:15–20). If we claim to be Christians but do not let Jesus's teachings guide our lives, we are nothing but hypocrites.

This does not deny the right of governments to maintain law and order and collect taxes. Jesus and other New Testament leaders supported the authority of civil governments (Matthew 22:15–22; Romans 13:1–7).

Biblical References
Proverbs 26:12; Isaiah 5:21; Matthew 7:1–5, 9:10–13, 18:10;
Luke 6:32–42, 7:36–50, 18:9–14; John 8:1–8, Romans 2:1–4,
3:23, 14:1,10–12; 1 Corinthians 4:5, 13:1–7, 16:14; Galatians
6:1–3; James 2:12–13, 4:11–12; 1 John 1:8

Don't Hold a Grudge

Jesus said there is no place for hatred, holding a grudge,
revenge, retaliation, or getting even in the life of a Christian.

> "You have heard that it was said, 'Eye for eye,
> and tooth for tooth.' But I tell you, Do not
> resist an evil person. If someone strikes you
> on the right cheek, turn to him the other also.
> And if someone wants to sue you and take
> your tunic, let him have your cloak as well …
> You have heard that it was said, 'Love your
> neighbor and hate your enemy.' But I tell you:
> Love your enemies and pray for those who
> persecute you, that you may be sons of your
> Father in heaven. He causes his sun to rise on
> the evil and the good, and sends rain on the
> righteous and the unrighteous." (Matthew 5:
> 38–40, 43–45 NIV)

Bearing a grudge and seeking revenge are never appropriate
responses to a perceived wrong. A grudge destroys the grudge-
holder with bitterness; revenge only escalates hostilities. Jesus

told us we must reconcile with our adversaries, forgive their transgressions, and let go of the anger that may tempt us to commit an act of revenge.

Biblical References
Leviticus 19:18; Psalm 37:8–9; Proverbs 10:12, 12:16, 15:1,7, 19:11, 20:22, 24:29; Matthew 5:21–26, 5:43–48, 12:17–21; 1 Corinthians 6:7–8; Ephesians 4:26, 31–32; Colossians 3:7–8; James 1:19–20; 1 Thessalonians 5:15; 1 Peter 3:9; 1 John 2:9–11, 4:19–21

Forgive Others

"If you forgive those who sin against you, your heavenly Father will forgive you. But if you refuse to forgive others, your Father will not forgive your sins" (Matthew 6:14–15 NLT).

Our merciful God forgives our sins and failings. In the same way, we must be merciful and forgive other people who sin against us or do us harm.

Recognizing the War

Before one can go into spiritual warfare, there must be recognition of the war. Sometimes you have those individuals who go into war not knowing why they are there, what they are fighting, or what they are fighting for.

This reflects many churchgoers who just go to church but truly have no idea of what's going on in the church. These are those peaceable worshipers who believe everything is going to be all right just because they went to church today. Then when the enemy shows up, they have no clue what to do. In turn, they are depressed, frustrated, and angry, being manipulated and set up by the enemy to do foolish things.

If we take a look at our military forces, we can learn some serious techniques and strategies that we may be able to instil in the believer.

The army of the Lord is not just some wacky platoon of soldiers running around playing good guy/bad guy. The army of the Lord should contain serious men and women of God ready to do whatever is commanded of them from their commanding officers. The army of the Lord chooses you; you don't choose it. And once you have been chosen and called to join this army, the commander-in-chief waits patiently for the called to answer to the call.

Contrary to popular belief, there are only two kinds of people on the planet. Though we have blacks, whites, Hispanics, Asians, and so many more cultures in our world, every culture and every individual of these cultures will fit into one of two categories. Either you are saved or you're not!

Either you are a Christian or you are a nonbeliever. God says either you are with me or you are against me. The greatest thing about the God we serve is that you don't have to stay on the outside of the fold. Confession, repentance, and believing Jesus died for your sin and rose on the third day will bring you into the family.

What actually is war? Why are we constantly fighting one another? If it's not this, it's that. Why can't we seek peace and live happily ever after? Matthew 10:34–36 (KJV) says,

> Think not that I am come to send peace on earth: I came not to send peace, but a sword. For I am come to set a man at variance against his father, and the daughter against her mother, and the daughter in law against her mother in law. And a man's foes shall be they of his own household.

Peace cannot exist between good and evil, God and Satan, Jesus Christ and the Antichrist, or the Holy Ghost and the False Prophet since Satan has declared war on God, proclaiming that he would exalt his throne above God's throne (Isaiah 14:12–14).

Now that war has been declared and the battle lines drawn, you must understand that it was not God declaring war. Satan declared war by turning against God and vowing he would build a kingdom better than the kingdom God already has.

Man has an inner compass that points us to God though. As believers, we must understand where the battle lines are drawn. If we misunderstand our limits, the enemy will use our ignorance to his advantage and destroy us and all those around us.

Once the believer understands the boundaries in Christ Jesus, we should then know where to go and not, who to hang around and not, and who to marry and not. As believers, we should work very hard at not crossing the line of unrighteousness but remain and maintain the boundary of righteousness.

Saying yes to the Lord is your enlistment process into the army of the Lord! There is no paperwork to sign because the Lord truly knows your heart and your intentions.

Psalm 44:21 (KJV) says, "Shall not God search this out? For he knoweth the secrets of the heart." It takes the power of the Holy Ghost to lose the proclamation of your mouth that Jesus is Lord!

1 Corinthians 12:3 (KJV) reads, "Wherefore I give you to understand, that no man speaking by the Spirit of God calleth Jesus accursed: and that no man can say that Jesus is the Lord, but by the Holy Ghost."

A basic training regimen for new believers is an area in the church, I personally believe, needs greater attention. To expect a baby Christian to go into war without the proper training is doing the church a grave injustice, and we can attribute the lack of spiritual training to be one of the reasons why many Christians backslide or fall prey to the enemy's ways.

We take the training process of many things in our lives very seriously; it's kind of odd to me how we can so easily overlook the most important training, the spiritual training that influences our lives.

Basic training is a crucial part of a believer's life because this is the part that redefines a Christian's life. The removal of the secular world can be trying and difficult in the beginning stages of a believer. But I truly believe this process is definitely necessary because we have relied upon the world for most of our needs, but now we must redefine in our spirits the true provider of all is God and not man.

In our military armed forces, upon a recruit's arrival to boot camp, they are stripped of everything civilian and then reissued everything military. We too as believers, if it were possible, should naturally go through a similar process, but since we are spiritual creatures when we become new believers, spiritually we should be stripped of our secular mind and reissued the mind that was also in Christ Jesus our Lord!

When you are issued all the things in which your country believes and all those around you have been issued the same underwear, uniform, and weapons, you are not only wearing what your country believes, you will begin to speak what your country speaks. You will start the process of becoming exactly what your country wants you to become.

Philippians 3:20 (KJV) says, "For our conversation is in heaven; from whence also we look for the Saviour, the Lord Jesus Christ."

Conversation
Politeuma – citizenship. If our citizenship is in heaven, then we should vow to defend our country.

Train Hard for What You Believe In; Spare No Pain to Achieve the Desired Gain!

Training for what you believe in is not an easy task. Let's face the facts: it's your spirit that wants to get closer to God, not your flesh. Matthew 26:41 (KJV) says, "Watch and pray, that ye enter not into temptation: the spirit indeed is willing, but the flesh is weak."

In order to whip yourself into shape, you must deny the flesh of its desires and focus on what it needs. As the body is exercised your spirit, man needs to exercise also. Basic training is the early stages of the believer's life, which means this is the time where they must be pushed harder than they have ever been.

They must be broken down and rebuilt again. All the things of the enemy must be removed and replaced with everything of God. Though this is a difficult task for today's Christian, it does not mean it is not needed.

We must emphasize the importance of pushing beyond our limits in order to attain all that God has for us. We serve a limitless God, so my question is: how in the world we can limit ourselves to the boundaries of this world?

When a soldier realizes that the United States of America is backing them up and realizes that no matter what goes down, when they need and call for backup, the United States of America is on its way. I'm sure that would give that soldier the confidence they may need to go into battle with any enemy!

It is very hard for Christians today to endure instructions; we for some reason already believe we know what to do in so many situations. Either we know more than the instructor or we show a serious attitude toward the one trying to teach, preach, or elevate us to the level to fight and maintain a battle.

Until the children of the Most High God can forget all about themselves and what they know, they can't be useful to God.

All that we know when we come to Christ will assist us in our ministries, never to take the lead position over the knowledge of God. God's word is not governed by what we know; the Word of God should govern what we know.

Paul said that I count all my knowledge as dung. Philippians 3:8 (KJV) says, "Yea doubtless, and I count all things but loss for the excellency of the knowledge of Christ Jesus my Lord: for whom I have suffered the loss of all things, and do count them but dung, that I may win Christ."

A major flaw we suffer from as believers is the inability to take a hit. I have watched Christians over and over again crumble at a single blow. I personally believe that if you don't like getting hit, then you should learn to duck occasionally, but quite honestly I don't care how many times you duck. Eventually you will get hit. Therefore, we must learn how to take a hit.

I'm not saying that we should just stand still and learn how to take blow after blow. But what I am saying is no matter how good or well prepared you are, you cannot avoid getting hit from time to time. It is imperative that, as believers, we learn how to take a blow or go with the blow to offset its potent power of destruction.

The body of Christ has lost the spirit of longevity, running as though this race is a sprint, forgetting it is a marathon. We must pace ourselves and run with a comfortable stride in order to maintain a good speed. Maintaining a good pace will put you in a good position to finish the race strong.

Contrary to what most do, it takes time to build up stamina. You must first start running with the mindset that you are running to build your endurance. You cannot run a mile when you first start running; you must build up your running by running little by little, maybe a lap at a time, until you build up stamina.

Please understand that running in a race is not the most important part of the race, but actually how you run a race. I have noticed for some years now that many believers start off running as though this race is a short one. Romans 10:2–3 (KJV) says, "For I bear them record that they have a zeal of God, but not according to knowledge. For they being ignorant of God's righteousness, and going about to establish their own righteousness, have not submitted themselves unto the righteousness of God."

God mandates that we bear the infirmities of the weak; instead I find a spirit of exploitation of the weak. Romans 15:1–2 (KJV) reads, "We then that are strong ought to bear the infirmities of the weak, and not to please ourselves. Let every one of us please his neighbour for his good to edification."

The word *army* is another word for team; we are workers together with God (2 Corinthians 6:1). We as believers must be able to depend on our fellow laborers in the vineyard. When I fall short, I need my fellow brethren to pick me up, not push me down. When this love is demonstrated among soldiers of the Lord, we will develop a ministry of reconciliation, not the ministry of scattering, separating, and destruction.

When we come together as one, we bring forth a oneness that pleases God. When we work together, fight together, and stand together, it is virtuously impossible for the enemy to defeat us. When we as believers stand shoulder to shoulder and back to back, we cover multiple directions of attacks, though the Bible says, "It is better to trust in the Lord than to put confidence in man" (Psalm 118:8 KJV).

We must come together as one. The unification of believers is a major power in the body of Christ.

Judges 20:11 (KJV) says, "So all the men of Israel were gathered against the city, knit together as one man." And Colossians 2:2 (KJV) reads, "That their hearts might be comforted, being knit together in love, and unto all riches of the full assurance of understanding, to the acknowledgement of the mystery of God, and of the Father, and of Christ."

The True War

Though we have been using our society's military forces as a natural guideline (Army, Navy, Air Force, and Marines), these tactics of preparation are just that, preparation and not actual combat.

Preparing for combat and actually engaging the enemy are two different things. The difficult task comes after all the basic training is over and you actually engage the enemy. I say this because no matter how much training you go through, what you truly need is a gift from God. What is that gift? Well, that gift is the Holy Ghost.

The Holy Spirit enhances all natural training, exercise, study, and self-improvements. This enhancement, empowering, and anointing is simply the power you will need to successfully implement all your training.

Spiritual things are of the spirit or nonmaterial. The word *spiritual* refers to nonmaterial things, including a spiritual body (1 Corinthians 15:44–46) and spiritual things as distinct from earthly goods (Romans 15:27; 1 Corinthians 9:11). But the most important use of the word refers to the Holy Spirit. The Spirit gave the law (Romans 7:14) and supplied Israel with water and food (1 Corinthians 10:3–4).

The Christian's very blessing is from the Spirit (Ephesians 1:3), as is his understanding of truth (1 Corinthians 2:13–15; Colossians 1:9). His songs should be sung in the Spirit (Ephesians 5:19; Colossians 3:16), and his ability to understand Scripture correctly is given by the Spirit (Revelation 11:8). He is to be so dominated by the Spirit that he can be called spiritual (1 Corinthians 2:15; Galatians 6:1) or, better yet, spiritually minded.

All these things are possible by the submission to God and the reception of His Holy Spirit. The Bible says in Acts 1:8 (KJV), "But ye shall receive power, after that the Holy Ghost is come upon you: and ye shall be witnesses unto me both in Jerusalem, and in all Judaea, and in Samaria, and unto the uttermost part of the earth."

The power you receive after the Holy Ghost has come upon you is the power to do God's will. Once you receive the Holy Spirit into your life, spiritual gifts are opened up to the believer. By virtue of the Holy Spirit, the believer is now opened to the new realm of the kingdom of God (John 3:3,5, 7:38–39).

This is where I would like to apply my focus, the new realm of the kingdom of God that the Holy Spirit opens up to the believer.

Spirit Identification

Understand that for the most part, demons are known by their primary names, which then identifies the functioning name the demon will specialize in once he becomes attached to a person, whether it be on the outside or inside of the person.

For instance, a spirit of lust will specialize in transmitting lust onto the person they are attached to. Once they transmit that feeling of lust onto this person, they will then try to get the person to act out on it. This is how many people end up engaging in fornication, adultery, or pornography. This is called "straight demonic persuasion" when a person gives way to these types of circumstances.

Most of these cases are not full possession type cases, so God will still hold the person completely responsible for their actions, even if a demon is covering them with this lustful feeling, along with providing them with the actual compulsion to try to act out on it. God still held both (Adam and Eve) totally responsible for their actions in the garden of Eden, even though the devil himself tempted Eve to eat the fruit from the forbidden tree, and then Eve persuaded Adam to do the same thing.

Satan still has not changed his tactics and strategies. He still uses both demons and other people to try to get us to fall into various types of sins. But whether we are coming under any kind of direct influence from demons or other people, the choice will always remain with us if we will fall for the temptation to sin directly against the Lord.

All demons can do is try to make you do bad and evil things. And unless you are dealing with a case of temporary possession or someone who has become mentally ill in some way, most of the time the person will have all of his senses fully intact enough to know right from wrong and will know what the full consequences of their acts will be if they decide to go all the way through with it.

A good example of this is the people who murder their loved ones in a fit of rage and jealousy. Most of the time, these crimes are premeditated, which means the person is actually thinking about it and planning on how to do it.

Once they go into this kind of a planning stage, the demons will then keep the pressure on from the back end to try to get them to follow all the way through it. But the person can still stop it and call it off anytime they want to. They know full well what the consequences are going to be if they get caught, life imprisonment or the death penalty. But in many of these cases, they will still follow all the way through with it and actually kill their spouse or whoever else they have targeted.

A primary demon's function names murder, rage, and hate are oftentimes the driving force behind these types of horrible crimes. But again, this person is still fully cooperating with these demons with their free will, and as a result, they will be held totally accountable and responsible by both the law if they are ever caught and by God Himself once they die and cross over to face Him head-on for their own personal judgment.

Most of the time, people have no idea that it really is demons that are operating behind the scenes, providing more fuel to their fires with what they specialize in, such as spirits of hate, murder, jealousy, rage, anger, bitterness, and the unforgiving spirit. Once a group of these types of demons attaches to a person who may have been really hurt in a love affair, a spouse being divorced by the other spouse, or a spouse catching another spouse in an adulterous love affair, they will then try to do everything they can to slime the person with what they specialize in to try to get them to act out on these negative feelings and emotions.

This is why it will really help when you know what some of the basic function names of the demons are, so you can then immediately spot their negative influence when they do try to move in for an attack on you or someone you know who may be open to their negative and evil influence.

**

The first basic rule of any type of warfare, whether it is spiritual or natural, is to know your enemy. And knowing the basic function names of the primary demons that are out there will give you a good head start, as their function names will tell you how they are playing that person, along with providing you with clues as to what their legal rights may be on that person.

Giving you some of the basic groupings will show you the different areas that demons like to target once they move in on a person and will enhance your basic training to be able to identify and eradicate any spiritual threat.

Here they are in a bolded, numbered format so you can have all of them right at your disposal.

1. Murder
2. The Occult
3. Lust
4. Pride
5. Mental Health
6. Unforgiveness
7. Sickness
8. Different Kinds of Vices
9. False Religions

These nine specific topics are some of the major areas that demons will try to target. These are the games that demons will try to play, and these are real life-and-death games, not fun-type games. This is why the Bible tells us to always be sober, vigilant, and alert for any kind of demonic activity that could set in on us or any of our close loved ones.

Here are the main groups and the function names of the demons operating in each of these specific groups. These demons are still to this day roaming in the air, trying to attack us anytime they see a hole occur in our protective hedge with the Lord. Also note that demons can play more than one of these games on any one individual person.

1. Murder

These types of demons and the ones who specialize in the occult are the worst types of demons you will ever encounter.

In this first group of demons, we will focus on demons that specialize in influencing people into a life of murder.

This will consist of demons that will attempt to influence people to either kill themselves in the form of a suicide or kill other people in cold-blooded murders. There is not a day that goes by where we do not see on the television or read in the newspapers about murder and suicide. The most heart-crushing fact is that it has become so common and widespread that we have become literally desensitized to all of it since we hear about it so much on a daily basis.

When it happens to someone who may be close to us, we are given the full realization of how evil of an act murder and suicide really is. And if it should happen to a very close loved one like your child, your spouse, or a parent, it will rip your heart into a million pieces and leave a hole in your soul that will never fully go away until you cross over to the other side to be with Jesus for all of eternity.

Through the power of the Holy Spirit on the inside of you, God can help heal the emotional wounds of this kind of trauma, but you will never lose the actual memory of the event or the sadness at losing a close loved one in such a horrible, evil, and senseless fashion.

The Bible has already given us fair warning that Satan and his demons have come to kill, steal, and destroy (John 10:10), and until Jesus comes back, we are all going to have to battle this kind of an evil reality regularly, whether we like it or not. So we must learn how the enemy works, strives, and diligently endeavors to operate against us so we know how to destroy him.

It's almost like watching a horror film. We sit through the whole movie watching the victims try to figure out how to destroy the monster that's trying to kill them. Toward the end of the movie, by some awesome revelation, someone in the movie comes up with the solution of how to kill the enemy. The funny thing about the film is that you probably figured out how to defeat the enemy by the middle of it, but you can't figure out how to defeat the devil in your own life. If you can sit attentively and watch the movie of your life, as you did the horror movie, you too will figure out how to defeat the enemy.

Again, here are some of the main primary names that demons function under that specialize in these kinds of extreme evil activity:

- Murder: The unlawful killing of one person by another, especially with premeditated malice. Matthew 19:18 (KJV) says, "He saith unto him, Which? Jesus said, Thou shalt do no murder, Thou shalt not commit adultery, Thou shalt not steal, Thou shalt not bear false witness."
- Hate: Strong dislike, disregard, or even indifference toward someone or something. 1 John 4:20 (KJV) says, "If a man say, I love God, and hateth his brother, he is a liar: for he that loveth not his brother whom he hath seen, how can he love God whom he hath not seen?"
- Rage: Violent and uncontrolled anger; a fit of violent wrath. Proverbs 6:34 (KJV), "For jealousy is the rage of a man: therefore he will not spare in the day of vengeance."

- Anger: The emotion of instant displeasure, which arises from the feeling of injury done or the discovery of injury intended or, in many cases, from the discovery of oversight of a supposed entitlement. Ephesians 4:31 (KJV) says, "Let all bitterness, and wrath, and anger, and clamor, and evil speaking, be put away from you, with all malice."

- Violence: The use of physical force, usually with an intent to violate or destroy. Violence is a violation of God's perfect order. Hebrews 11:34 (KJV) says, "Quenched the violence of fire, escaped the edge of the sword, out of weakness were made strong, waxed valiant in fight, turned to flight the armies of the aliens."

- Death: A term which, when applied to the lower orders of living things such as plants and animals, means the end of life. Concerning human beings, however, death is not the end of life. The Bible teaches that man is more than a physical creature; he is also a spiritual being. For man, therefore, physical death does not mean the end of existence but the end of life as we know it and the transition to another dimension in which our conscious existence continues. 1 John 3:14 (KJV) says, "We know that we have passed from death unto life, because we love the brethren. He that loveth not his brother abideth in death."

- Revenge: Inflicting punishment or harm on another to pay back for an injury or insult. 2 Corinthians 10:6 (KJV) says, "And having in a readiness to revenge all disobedience, when your obedience is fulfilled."

- Destruction: The state or fact of being destroyed; ruin; destroy; to ruin the structure, organic existence, or condition of; to ruin as if by tearing to shreds. John 10:10 (KJV) says, "The thief cometh not, but for to steal, and to kill, and to destroy: I am come that they might have life, and that they might have it more abundantly."

- Darkness: The absence of light. Darkness existed before the light of creation (Genesis 1:2). John 12:35 (KJV) says, "Then Jesus said unto them, Yet a little while is the light with you. Walk while ye have the light, lest darkness come upon you: for he that walketh in darkness knoweth not whither he goeth."

- Suicide: the killing of one's self with malice aforethought and while in the possession of a sound mind (a form of murder; the murdering of oneself).

- Abortion: The termination of a pregnancy after, accompanied by, resulting in, or closely followed by the death of the embryo or fetus; as a spontaneous expulsion of a human fetus. Jeremiah 1:5 (KJV) says, "Before I formed thee in the belly I knew thee; and before thou camest forth out of the womb I sanctified thee, and I ordained thee a prophet unto the nations."

- Jealousy: Hostile toward an adversary, contender, or challenger; one believed to enjoy an advantage over another. Proverbs 6:34 (KJV) says, "For jealousy is the rage of a man: therefore he will not spare in the day of vengeance."

- Sadism: A sexual perversion in which gratification is obtained by the infliction of physical or mental pain on others; a delight in cruelty; excessive cruelty. Pleasure and pain are opposites; sadism attempts to bring them together for sexual gratification. Pain is a side effect or an offshoot of sin. Genesis 3:16–17 (KJV) says, "Unto the woman he said, I will greatly multiply thy sorrow and thy conception; in sorrow thou shalt bring forth children; and thy desire shall be to thy husband, and he shall rule over thee. And unto Adam he said, Because thou hast hearkened unto the voice of thy wife, and hast eaten of the tree, of which I commanded thee, saying, Thou shalt not eat of it: cursed is the ground for thy sake; in sorrow shalt thou eat of it all the days of thy life."

- Fighting: To contend in battle or physical combat; to strive to overcome a person by blows or weapons. Deuteronomy 3:22 (KJV) says, "Ye shall not fear them: for the Lord your God he shall fight for you."

As it has been said before, demons usually travel in groups or clusters, with one demon being the chief demon and the rest being his minions under his direct control and direction. In many of these cases, the chief demon will be a spirit of murder, and his minions will have some of the function names listed previously. They will then move in and set up shop on someone if they have the appropriate legal rights to be able to do so. They will then try to work and play that person over a period of time to either try to get them to kill themselves or other people (or both, as murder-suicides are still very common in this day and age).

Again, in most of these cases, the person is not in a fully possessed state. They still have most, if not all, of their senses fully intact and know basic right from wrong. The demons will then plant in their thoughts, their suggestions, their pictures in their mind's eye, and their strategies on how to do this, but the person can still resist these types of evil temptations at any time and choose not to act out on them.

Demons cannot make you do anything against your own free will. All they can do is try to persuade you to do it, along with try to give you the actual desire and compulsion to want to do it. From there, the choice will be up to that person as to whether or not they will want to go all the way through with it and actually act out on these evil desires that the demons are implanting into them.

This is why it is said the battle is in the mind. Because of the targeted area (the mind), we must learn not only how to fight but where the fight is located. And the battle is in the mind. "Casting down imaginations, and every high thing that exalteth itself against the knowledge of God, and bringing into captivity every thought to the obedience of Christ" (2 Corinthians 10:5 KJV).

It would be awfully silly to run into battle fully armored, fully skilled in war tactics, and fully ready to engage the enemy and show up at the wrong battle location. Can you imagine a dear family member calling you for help and you saying "I am on my way to assist in your dilemma" and when you get there no one is there? Your intentions were great, and you truly meant to help, but how can you help or fight in the war if you keep showing up to the wrong place for the battle?

So one of the most effective weapons the enemy has is confusion; his power to distract is great, and he uses it to keep our mind from focusing on God so he can confuse us and then lead us through false persuasion.

It simply amazes me how so many people will blindly follow these kinds of evil demonic suggestions and promptings and actually carry out acts of pure, cold-blooded murders on either themselves or anyone else the demons have targeted for them. Just because you get an evil thought or desire to kill either yourself or someone else, this does not mean that you have to actually try to carry it out.

Again, people need to be taught the basics of how demons will try to play mind games so they can get you to do their evil bidding. The mind is the battlefield in the area of spiritual warfare, with both demons and God trying to influence you. God tries to transform and renew your mind through His Word; demons try to reach your mind so they can get you to act out on their evil suggestions.

2. The Occult

The demons we will deal with next are some of the worst you can ever come across. Many deliverance ministers have found out on the actual battlefields that demons who specialize in any area of the occult are some of the more evil and powerful demons in Satan's kingdom and sometimes are the hardest to actually cast out. This is why God the Father was so strict back in the Old Testament with the Jewish people in that they were to have absolutely nothing to do with any kind of occult activity.

It's believed that there are demons that literally specialize in every single kind of occult activity out there. The following is a list of different kinds of occult activities that we are to stay completely away from in our life:

1. Fortune-telling of any kind (e.g., palm reading, crystal ball gazing, numerology, or seeing psychics [i.e., predicting the future through magic and enchantment]). At Philippi, the apostle Paul healed a slave girl who had brought her masters much profit by fortune-telling (Acts 16:16; KJV soothsaying).

2. Tarot cards. Any of a set of usually seventy-eight playing cards, including twenty-two pictorial cards used for fortune-telling.

3. Ouija boards and automatic writing. A board with the alphabet and other signs on it that is used to seek spiritualistic or telepathic messages.

4. Séances and any involvement with mediums or spiritists. A person thought to have the power to communicate with the spirits of the dead (Isaiah 8:19, 19:3, 29:4). According to the law of Moses, anyone who professed to be a medium or channel of communication to the spirit world was to be put to death by stoning (Leviticus 20:27).

5. Astrology and any form of horoscopes. The study of the sun, moon, planets, and stars in the belief that they influence individuals and the course of human events. Astrology attempts to predict the future by analyzing the movements of these heavenly bodies. Although

the word *astrology* does not appear in the Bible, the word *astrologers* does. The prophet Isaiah taunted the Babylonians to go to the powerless "astrologers, the stargazers, and the monthly prognosticators" (Isaiah 47:13) for their salvation. The word is found eight times in the book of Daniel in association with *magicians, sorcerers, Chaldeans, wise men,* and *soothsayers* (Daniel 1:20, 2:2,10,27, 4:7, 5:7,11,15).

6. I Ching. Also known as the Classic of Changes or the Book of Changes. This ancient Chinese book contains a divination system that has been used for more than five thousand years as an aid to making decisions, predicting the future, and so forth. So if nothing else, it is a long-standing and popular source of wisdom and inspiration.

7. Hypnotism. A trancelike state that resembles sleep but is induced by a person whose suggestions are readily accepted by the subject. The fruit of the Spirit is self-control (Galatians 5:22–23). As we follow the Spirit's lead, He will give us the power to better control our own selves. Hypnosis involves the transfer of control away from ourselves to another person.

8. Transcendental meditation (TM) or any type of Far Eastern meditation. A technique of rendering the mind passive as one seeks to turn off all thoughts and images. But Christian meditative prayer and reflection make the mind and spirit active as the believer seeks to deepen his appreciation of, and commitment to, Christ as Lord. The Christian's meditation is part of

a personal relationship with the Lord, while TM is impersonal in nature. Joshua 1:8 (KJV) reads, "This book of the law shall not depart out of thy mouth; but thou shalt meditate therein day and night, that thou mayest observe to do according to all that is written therein: for then thou shalt make thy way prosperous, and then thou shalt have good success."

9. Crystals. A clear, glasslike object that may come in different shades of colors, like a precious stone used as a healing stone through some sort of mystical power. Ezekiel 13:18, 20, 21 shares with us that God is not pleased with those who tie these charms to their wrist to entice others to follow its charm.

10. Witchcraft. The use of sorcery or magic; communication with the devil or a familiar. It is one of the works of the flesh (Galatians 5:20), which truly displeases God.

11. Satanism. The worship of Satan marked by the mockery of Christian rites. Exodus 34:14 (KJV) reads, "For thou shalt worship no other god: for the Lord, whose name is Jealous, is a jealous God."

12. Voodoo. A religion derived from African polytheism and ancestor worship. It is practiced chiefly in Haiti. It is a person who deals in spells and necromancy and sorcerer's spells.

13. Channeling. To serve as a channeler or intermediary for spirits. Leviticus 19:31 (KJV) says, "Regard not them that have familiar spirits, neither seek after wizards, to be defiled by them: I am the Lord your God."

14. Reincarnation. A rebirth in a new body or forms of life; a rebirth of a soul in a new human body; a fresh embodiment. Ecclesiastes 12:7 (KJV) states, "Then shall the dust return to the earth as it was: and the spirit shall return unto God who gave it."

15. Astral projection. An induced out-of-body experience. Ecclesiastes 3:2 (KJV) says, "A time to be born, and a time to die; a time to plant, and a time to pluck up that which is planted." In other words, God is saying, "I put your spirit in your body, and it will stay there until I am ready for to come out!"

16. Extrasensory perception (ESP). Perception, as in telepathy, clairvoyance, and precognition, that involves awareness of information about events external to the self not gained through the senses and not deducible from previous experience.

17. Dungeons and Dragons. A medieval-type of role-playing game imitating sorcerers and wizards, mystical time imitators.

18. New Age movement techniques and activities. A modern revival of ancient religious traditions, along with a potpourri of influences: Eastern mysticism, modern philosophy and psychology, science and science fiction, and the counterculture of the 1950s and 1960s. New Age is not new. "So here we are in the New Age, a combination of spirituality and superstition, fad and farce, about which the only thing certain is that it, is not new." Colossians 2:8 (KJV) says, "Beware lest any man spoil you through

philosophy and vain deceit, after the tradition of men, after the rudiments of the world, and not after Christ."

19. Necromancy. Conjuration of the spirits of the dead for purposes of magically revealing the future or influencing the course of events; magic; sorcery.

Again, we cannot emphasize strongly enough that both believers and nonbelievers alike stay completely away from this kind of demonic activity. Every single one of the above activities has specific demons assigned to them, and they will come directly after you if you attempt to try any of them.

3. Lust

The next class of demon we will deal with have perhaps been guilty of bringing down more present-day ministries than all of the other ones combined, especially with men. These types of demons are also responsible for the different kinds of perversions and filth we see running across every segment of our society today.

Here is a basic list of some of these kinds of demons:

- Lust: Desire for what is forbidden; an obsessive sexual craving. Titus 2:12 (KJV) says, "Teaching us that, denying ungodliness and worldly lusts, we should live soberly, righteously, and godly, in this present world."
- Fornication: Sexual relationships outside the bonds of marriage. 1 Corinthians 5:11 (KJV) says, "But now I have written unto you not to keep company,

if any man that is called a brother be a fornicator, or covetous, or an idolater, or a railer, or a drunkard, or an extortioner; with such an one no not to eat."

- Adultery: Willful sexual intercourse with someone other than one's spouse. Jesus expanded the meaning of adultery to include the cultivation of lust, "Whoever looks at a woman to lust for her has already committed adultery with her in his heart" (Matthew 5:28 KJV).

- Pornography: Material (e.g., books, photographs, or movies) that depicts erotic behavior and is intended to cause sexual excitement. James 1:14–15 (KJV) says, "But every man is tempted, when he is drawn away of his own lust, and enticed. Then when lust hath conceived, it bringeth forth sin: and sin, when it is finished, bringeth forth death."

- Pedophilia: Sexual perversion in which children are the preferred sexual object. 2 Peter 2:9 (KJV) says, "The Lord knoweth how to deliver the godly out of temptations, and to reserve the unjust unto the day of judgment to be punished."

- Rape: The crime of forcing another person to submit to sexual intercourse. Hebrews 3:8 (KJV) states, "Harden not your hearts, as in the provocation, in the day of temptation in the wilderness."

- Incest: Sexual relations with near kin, a sin expressly forbidden by the law of Moses. Leviticus 20:12 (KJV) says, "And if a man lie with his daughter in law, both of them shall surely be put to death: they have wrought confusion; their blood shall be upon them."

- Homosexuality: A person who is attracted sexually to members of their own sex. The apostle Paul listed homosexuals among "the unrighteous" who would not inherit the kingdom of God. 1 Corinthians 6:9 (KJV) states, "Know ye not that the unrighteous shall not inherit the kingdom of God? Be not deceived: neither fornicators, nor idolaters, nor adulterers, nor effeminate, nor abusers of themselves with mankind."

- Transvestism: A person, especially a male, who adopts the dress and often the behavior typical of the opposite sex, especially for purposes of emotional or sexual gratification. Deuteronomy 22:5 (KJV) says, "The woman shall not wear that which pertaineth unto a man, neither shall a man put on a woman's garment: for all that do so are abomination unto the Lord thy God."

- Transsexuality: A person who psychologically identifies with the opposite sex and may seek to live as a member of this sex, especially by undergoing surgery and hormone therapy to obtain the necessary physical appearance (as by changing the external sex organs). Psalm 139:14 (KJV) states, "I will praise thee; for I am fearfully and wonderfully made: marvellous are thy works; and that my soul knoweth right well."

- Sexual orgies: A sexual encounter involving many people; an excessive sexual indulgence. God forbids fornication and adultery; multiple sex partners are even more included (1 Corinthians 5:11).

- Wife swapping: Sharing one's wife with another for sexual pleasure. Titus 1:6 says, "If any be blameless, the husband of one wife, having faithful children not accused of riot or unruly."
- Prostitution: The act or practice of promiscuous sexual relations, especially for money.
- Bestiality: The practice of sexual activity between humans and non-humans (animals). Leviticus 18:23 (KJV) says, "Neither shalt thou lie with any beast to defile thyself therewith: neither shall any woman stand before a beast to lie down thereto: it is confusion."
- Sadomasochism: The source of pleasure from the infliction of physical or mental pain either on others or on oneself.

All of these forbidden areas with the Lord have one major thing in common, that they are all tied into a spirit of lust, a spirit of sexual arousal where the ultimate aim is for some kind of sexual gratification.

If you will notice, all of these kinds of activities have our sexuality tied into the wrong kinds of targets. God Himself created us with the ability to have sexual thoughts and feelings, but this gift was only meant to be used and shared within the confines of a holy heterosexual marriage, not in the kinds of aberrant activities listed previously.

Demons obviously know we have this kind of incredible gift from the Lord, so they will do everything they can to try to get you to release this gift through the wrong kinds of targets and activities such as the ones listed before. How many marriages, ministries, and personal lives have been totally destroyed and brought down as a result of people following after the different kinds of spirits of lust?

The strongest man in God to have probably ever lived, Samson, was completely brought down as a result of lusting after the wrong kind of woman. And to this very day, many people still have not learned from the past and how deadly this kind of spirit can be.

The smartest man who ever lived, Solomon, was completely brought down as a result of lusting after the wrong women. And again to this very day, many people still have not learned from the past and how deadly this kind of spirit can be.

We still have many married people across the world who are cheating on their spouses in their marriages. And then to top it off, we still have to deal with all of the rapists and pedophiles who are out there, preying on our young children and women, all because they are choosing with their own free wills not to try to fight this kind of bad and evil spirit.

4. Pride

Satan himself is a perfect example of someone who fell from grace and favor with the Lord as a result of too much pride being built up in his personality over a certain period of time.

Once too much pride starts to build up over time in your personality, you will then start to lose your ability to see what the real truth is in many of the important matters in your life. The only truth you will now see is what you think the truth is, even if that truth goes against God Almighty Himself.

You will then start to become a little god yourself, thinking that all of the world revolves around you and your own set agendas. You will then become very selfish and narcissistic and will refuse to listen to any kind of correction or counsel the Lord will try to bring your way.

Demons know how powerful and destructive of a thing pride can be in helping to bring a person down, so they will do everything they can behind the scenes to try to build up a person's ego through false flattery and vain imaginations.

Here is a list of some of the diverse kinds of demons who will try to bring someone down through the spirit of pride:

- Pride: An unwarranted and perverse self-esteem, attended with disrespect and rude treatment of others. Proverbs 16:18 (KJV) says, "Pride goeth before destruction, and an haughty spirit before a fall."
- Arrogance: An attitude of superiority manifested in an overbearing manner or in conceited claims or assumptions. Proverbs 29:23 (TEV) reads, "Arrogance will bring your downfall, but if you are humble, you will be respected."
- Haughtiness: Deliberately and scornfully proud. Proverbs 18:12 (KJV) states, "Before destruction the heart of man is haughty, and before honour is humility."
- Rebellion: Opposition to one in authority or dominance. 1 Samuel 15:23 (KJV) says, "For rebellion is as the sin of witchcraft, and stubbornness is as iniquity and idolatry. Because thou hast rejected the word of the Lord, he hath also rejected thee from being king."

- Blasphemy: The act of cursing, slandering, reviling, or showing contempt or lack of reverence for God. Matthew 12:31 (KJV) states, "Wherefore I say unto you, All manner of sin and blasphemy shall be forgiven unto men: but the blasphemy against the Holy Ghost shall not be forgiven unto men."

- Control, Domination: Supremacy or preeminence over another; exercise of mastery or ruling power; exercising governing or controlling influence. Philippians 2:3 (KJV) reads, "Let nothing be done through strife or vainglory; but in lowliness of mind let each esteem other better than themselves."

- Possessiveness: Manifesting possession or the desire to own or dominate another; jealousy. Proverbs 6:34 (KJV) says, "For jealousy is the rage of a man: therefore he will not spare in the day of vengeance."

- Contention: A point advanced or maintained in a debate or argument; rivalry; competition. Proverbs 13:10 (KJV) states, "Only by pride cometh contention: but with the well advised is wisdom."

- Quarreling: To find fault; to contend or dispute actively; usually a verbal conflict among antagonists. Colossians 3:13 (KJV) says, "Forbearing one another, and forgiving one another, if any man have a quarrel against any: even as Christ forgave you, so also do ye."

- Critical, Judgmental: Relating to or involving judgment; characterized by a tendency to judge harshly. Matthew 7:1–2 (KJV) states, "Judge not, that ye be not judged. For with what judgment ye judge, ye shall be judged: and with what measure ye mete, it shall be measured to you again."

- Selfish: An unreasonable self-love, prompting one for the sake of personal gratification or advantage, to disregarding the rights and feelings of others. Philippians 2:3–4 (TLB) states, "Don't be selfish; don't live to make a good impression on others. Be humble, thinking of others as better than yourself. Don't just think about your own affairs, but be interested in others, too, and in what they are doing."

- Narcissistic: Egoism; egocentrism; love of or sexual desire for one's own body. 2 Timothy 3:1–7 (KJV) reads, "This know also, that in the last days perilous times shall come. For men shall be lovers of their own selves, covetous, boasters, proud, blasphemers, disobedient to parents, unthankful, unholy, Without natural affection, trucebreakers, false accusers, incontinent, fierce, despisers of those that are good, Traitors, heady, highminded, lovers of pleasures more than lovers of God; Having a form of godliness, but denying the power thereof: from such turn away. For of this sort are they which creep into houses, and lead captive silly women laden with sins, led away with divers lusts, Ever learning, and never able to come to the knowledge of the truth."

- Unbelief: Lack of belief or faith in God and His provision. While unbelief does not hinder God's faithfulness, it does affect the individual's capacity to receive the benefits of that faithfulness. Romans 3:3

(KJV) asks, "For what if some did not believe? shall their unbelief make the faith of God without effect?"

- Skepticism: An attitude of doubt or a disposition of uncertainty harboring suspicion either in general or toward a particular object. Mark 11:23 (KJV) states, "For verily I say unto you, That whosoever shall say unto this mountain, Be thou removed, and be thou cast into the sea; and shall not doubt in his heart, but shall believe that those things which he saith shall come to pass; he shall have whatsoever he saith."

- Greed: A selfish and excessive desire for more of something (e.g., money) than needed. Proverbs 15:27 (KJV) says, "He that is greedy of gain troubleth his own house; but he that hateth gifts shall live."

- Paranoia: A psychosis characterized by systematized delusions of persecution; a tendency on the part of an individual or group toward excessive or irrational suspiciousness and distrustfulness of others. Proverbs 3:5–6 (KJV) says, "Trust in the Lord with all thine heart; and lean not unto thine own understanding. In all thy ways acknowledge him, and he shall direct thy paths."

- Deceit: The act or practice of deceiving; deception; an attempt or device to deceive; trick; the quality of being deceitful; mockery. Proverbs 12:20 (KJV) states, "Deceit is in the heart of them that imagine evil: but to the counsellors of peace is joy."

Once the spirit of pride enters into someone, either through demons and/or a person's own human spirit, many of these characteristics will follow right along with it. How many prideful people do you know who also show signs of additional negative traits, such as being too judgmental and too critical of other people? Since their inflated sense of pride tells them they are always right and never wrong, then there is no room for anyone else who does not agree with them. As a result, they will become very judgmental and critical of anyone else who does not agree with them.

As their pride continues to build up, they will then become more selfish and self-absorbed, as all they will be able to see what is in their own little world. As a result, everything else in their lives will become totally unrelated, including the members of their own families.

They will then start to want more and more, especially in the area of power, wealth, authority, control, money, and material goods. From there a strong spirit of greed will start to enter in, and before you know it, they will have lost all contact with God, their best friends, and family members. They will then become an island and a god all to themselves.

And then it happens. Everything comes tumbling down around them. They lose all of their friends, families, wealth, and money. And most importantly of all, they lose their connection and personal relationship to God Himself.

Demons are masters at playing the pride game with people since that is what caused all of them to get cast out of heaven in the first place. And so many people to this very day are still continuing to fall for this type of evil spirit, such as some of our politicians, CEOs of different companies, and even some of the pastors and clergy in our different churches.

Just realize that pride is a major, offensive weapon of demons and they will play this kind of game with anyone they feel will be susceptible to it, especially those in any type of leadership position or desires to be in a leadership position.

5. Mental Health

The Holy Bible shares with us that God has given us a spirit of power, love, and a "sound mind." And because of this power, the enemy launches a great attack. One of the major demonic attacks we as believers are faced with is demons trying to crack our mental stability. This is achieved by demons working diligently to distract our focus by getting our eyes off the Lord in order to give us an unsound mind. In other words, they will try to make us mentally unstable as much as they can. 2 Timothy 1:7 (KJV) says, "For God has not given us a spirit of fear, but of power and of love and of a sound mind."

Demonic mind games are one of the demons' favorite games to play. If they can make us mentally unstable to any significant degree, they will then be able to do significant damage to our abilities to operate in our callings, possibly knocking us completely out of our calls. Here are some of the functioning names that demons operate under in this realm:

- Fear: An unpleasant, often strong, emotion caused by anticipation or awareness of danger. Matthew 10:28 (KJV) says, "And fear not them which kill the body, but are not able to kill the soul: but rather fear him which is able to destroy both soul and body in hell."

- Depression: A state of feeling sad; a psychoneurotic or psychotic disorder marked especially by sadness, inactivity, difficulty in thinking and concentration, or a significant increase or decrease in appetite and time spent sleeping; feelings of misery and hopelessness and sometimes suicidal tendencies. Psalm 3:3 (KJV) reads, "Lord, how are they increased that trouble me! Many are they that rise up against me."

- Torment: To inflict physical pain or mental agony. Revelation 21:4 (KJV) states, "And God shall wipe away all tears from their eyes; and there shall be no more death, neither sorrow, nor crying, neither shall there be any more pain: for the former things are passed away."

- Dread: To fear greatly; to feel extreme reluctance to meet or face. 1 Chronicle 22:13 (KJV) reads, "Then shalt thou prosper, if thou takest heed to fulfil the statutes and judgments which the Lord charged Moses with concerning Israel: be strong, and of good courage; dread not, nor be dismayed."

- Hopelessness: Having no expectation of good or success; giving no ground for hope. 1 Peter 1:13 (KJV) states, "Wherefore gird up the loins of your mind, be sober, and hope to the end for the grace that is to be brought unto you at the revelation of Jesus Christ."

- Despair: To lose all hope or confidence; to lose hope for. 2 Corinthians 4:8 (KJV) says, "We are troubled on every side, yet not distressed; we are perplexed, but not in despair."

- Insecurity: Not confident or sure; uncertain; not highly stable or well-adjusted; lacking in assurance. Philippians 1:6 (KJV) tells us, "Being confident of this very thing, that he which hath begun a good work in you will perform it until the day of Jesus Christ."

- Paranoia: A psychosis characterized by systematized delusions of persecution; a tendency on the part of an individual or group toward excessive or irrational suspiciousness and distrustfulness of others. Proverbs 3:5–6 (KJV) says, "Trust in the Lord with all thine heart; and lean not unto thine own understanding. In all thy ways acknowledge him, and he shall direct thy paths."

- Suspicion: Imagining evil of others without proof; the act or instance of suspecting something wrong without proof or slight evidence. Exodus 20:16 (KJV) states, "Thou shalt not bear false witness against thy neighbour."

- Distrust: The lack or absence of trust; to have no trust or confidence in. Proverbs 3:5–6 (KJV) reads, "Trust in the Lord with all thine heart; and lean not unto thine own understanding. 6 In all thy ways acknowledge him, and he shall direct thy paths."

- Loneliness: Being without company; cut off from others; not frequented by human beings; sad from being alone; producing a feeling of bleakness or unhappiness. John 16:32 (KJV) says, "Behold, the hour cometh, yea, is now come, that ye shall be scattered, every man to his own, and shall leave me alone: and yet I am not alone, because the Father is with me."

- Shyness: Easily frightened; timid; likely to avoid a person or thing; hesitant in committing oneself; reserved; secluded; hidden. 1 Thessalonians 2:2 (KJV) states, "But even after that we had suffered before, and were shamefully entreated, as ye know, at Philippi, we were bold in our God to speak unto you the gospel of God with much contention."

- Discouragement: To deprive of courage or confidence; dishearten; to hinder by disfavoring. Joshua 1:9–10 (KJV) reads, "Have not I commanded thee? Be strong and of a good courage; be not afraid, neither be thou dismayed: for the Lord thy God is with thee whithersoever thou goest. Then Joshua commanded the officers of the people."

- Passivity: Lacking in energy or will; not active or operating; receiving impression from external agents; not acting; being the objective of the action rather than the subject. A passive mind doesn't completely accept that God's Word is true; therefore it is always puzzled and speculative. These perplexities and speculations deteriorate the will, enabling a person to be slow to obey God. This is the cause of most of the instability we see in Christians today. It causes us to be unsettled in our minds. God's purpose within is to establish and settle us. 1 Peter 5:6–11 (KJV) says, "If we refuse to stand against the devil, God cannot strengthen us." Mental passivity includes in its descriptive words:

unreasoning, inactive, unenthusiastic, unresponsive, unqualified obedience to the commands of another, lawful, or unlawful. (Mark 4:24 [KJV]: futile mind; Ephesians 4:17–19 [KJV]: seducing pastors or teachers who patronize you to get you on their side, many times opposing God's word; Romans 6:16 [KJV]: You will become the slave of whomever you yield your mind to obey.) A person who does not successfully complete earthly duties shows mental passivity.

- Lying: Any statement or act designed to deceive another person. The motivation for most lying is a desire either to hurt the one against whom the lie is directed (Romans 3:13) or to protect oneself, usually out of fear or pride. Ephesians 4:25 (KJV) says, "Wherefore putting away lying, speak every man truth with his neighbour: for we are members one of another."

- Deceit: To be false; to cause to accept as true or valid what is false or invalid. Jeremiah 17:9 (KJV) states, "The heart is deceitful above all things, and desperately wicked: who can know it?" Deceit is trickery and dishonesty. Satan is the father of deceit.

- Antisocial: Averse to the society of others; hostile or harmful to organized society; especially being or marked by behavior deviating sharply from the social norm.

- Compulsive neurotic behavior: An emotionally unstable individual; having power to compel; relating to, caused by, or suggestive of psychological compulsion or obsession. James 1:8 (KJV) reads, "A double minded man is unstable in all his ways."

- Phobias: An exaggerated usually inexplicable and illogical fear of a particular object, class of objects, or situation. Fear is a feeling of reverence, awe, and respect or an unpleasant emotion caused by a sense of danger. 2 Timothy 1:7 (KJV) says, "For God hath not given us the spirit of fear; but of power, and of love, and of a sound mind."

- Madness: The quality or state of being mad; rage; insanity; extreme folly. Luke 6:11 (KJV) states, "And they were filled with madness; and communed one with another what they might do to Jesus."

- Insanity: A deranged state of the mind, usually occurring as a specific disorder (e.g., schizophrenia). Luke 8:35 (KJV) tells us, "Then they went out to see what was done; and came to Jesus, and found the man, out of whom the devils were departed, sitting at the feet of Jesus, clothed, and in his right mind: and they were afraid."

- Schizophrenia: A psychotic disorder characterized by loss of contact with the environment by noticeable deterioration in the level of functioning in everyday life. Matthew 6:24 (KJV) says, "No man can serve two masters: for either he will hate the one, and love the other; or else he will hold to the one, and despise the other. Ye cannot serve God and mammon."

- Multiple personalities: A hysterical neurosis in which the personality becomes dissociated into two or more distinct but complex and socially and behaviorally integrated parts each of which becomes dominant and controls behavior from time to time to the exclusion of the others. James 1:8 (KJV) reads, "A double minded man is unstable in all his ways."

- Hearing voices: To receive communication, perceptions, and apprehensions listening to two or more voices. John 10:27 (KJV) says, "My sheep hear my voice, and I know them, and they follow me." And John 10:5 (KJV) states, "And a stranger will they not follow, but will flee from him: for they know not the voice of strangers."

- Mind control: The elements of an individual that feels, perceives, thinks, wills, and especially reasons; another commands him. Romans 6:16 (KJV) reads, "Know ye not, that to whom ye yield yourselves servants to obey, his servants ye are to whom ye obey; whether of sin unto death, or of obedience unto righteousness?"

Many of us occasionally fight with some of these types of faults and imperfections. Not everyone who has fear, shyness, or loneliness on them is under any kind of demonic attack. But where you can get into problems with some of these types of conditions is when demons do move in and try to intensify what you may already be going through.

For example, if you are combating your own personal emotions of fear and lack of confidence as a consequence of having just lost your job, family, health, or anything that can rock your world, then the demon will try to fasten himself to you and intensify the fear factor by hitting you with his own fears. Once the demon begins to implement his fear, which is added to your own fears, you are now dealing with natural and spiritual fears, which can totally overwhelm you when you're not even prepared to deal with your own fears.

A demon and his evil forces are always searching for an opening in the defensive lines of a believer, constantly searching for a crack in the shield of faith so he can slide doubt in as to diminish your faith. If they see that you are battling any type of abnormal fear for any type of crisis you are going through, they will then try to add to it so they can get you paralyzed. And if you get paralyzed enough, you will stop trying to move forward. And if you stop trying to move forward, you may end up handcuffing God in being able to work with you. This is why it is so important that you realize the types of games that demons are capable of playing with you so you do not fall into their traps.

The demonic forces we battle daily are not equipped to stop us due to the limited resources that demons have in their attacks on the believer. To be honest, we are our worst enemy.

Isaiah 54:17 (KJV) says, "No weapon that is formed against thee shall prosper; and every tongue that shall rise against thee in judgment thou shalt condemn. This is the heritage of the servants of the Lord, and their righteousness is of me, saith the Lord."

1 John 4:4 (KJV) states, "Ye are of God, little children, and have overcome them: because greater is he that is in you, than he that is in the world."

So remember, the devil can't stop you. At best he may slow you down but never stop you. There is only one person on this planet who can stop you, you. These demonic forces will not only try to influence you, but they will also try to influence those around you and these individuals around you who allow these demons to use them. These demonic forces use these haters and hinderers to agitate you to the point of giving up.

We forget so quickly the instructions of our Lord and Savior Jesus Christ, who says to pray for them that despitefully use you. Jesus also says to pray for your enemy. Though these holy statements are looked upon as a natural difficulty, all things are possible to them that believe.

If you have just lost your job, family, or health, you will need to seek ye first the kingdom of God because as you begin to search out for a new job, an intimate relationship with another human being, or direction in your health issues, God will fully guide your steps into the next new stage in your life. But if you quit seeking after that next stage of life due to battling too much fear and insecurity, then God may not be able to lead you to that next place in your life because you have just taken yourself off His playing field. And that is exactly what the demons will try to do to you, knock you right off the playing field and onto the bench, so God will not be able to use you or work with you.

Again, do not fall for these kinds of tricks and traps from these demons. This is why the Bible tells us that having knowledge can help keep us from being destroyed and going into any type of captivity. And if the demons can start to play this kind of mind game with you where they can get you mentally unstable to any kind of a significant degree, then you will go into a certain amount of mental captivity. And that certain amount of mental captivity could then end up freezing and paralyzing you and keep you from being able to progress any further on the divine path that God has you set up on.

If demons cannot kill you, they will then try to paralyze you so you can no longer move forward and function in the calling that God has set up for your life. That is why having some semblance of a good, sound mind in this life will really help you in being able to fully complete your call for the Lord. Demons know this, and that is why they will try to infect you with some of the above-mentioned negative qualities.

6. Unforgiveness

Another major area that demons will try to target once they see this kind of an opening in your defenses is in the area of unforgiveness. They will try and target this specific area is due to Mark 11:25 (KJV), "AND WHENEVER YOU STAND PRAYING, if you have anything against anyone, forgive him, that your Father in heaven may also forgive you your trespasses. But if you do not forgive, neither will your Father in heaven forgive your trespasses."

Not only does this verse tell us that God will not be forgiving of all of our trespasses if we do not forgive the ones who have trespassed against us, but this verse is also implying that we may have a very hard time getting any of our personal prayers answered with Him, as it starts with the specific wording, "And whenever you stand praying."

And if you cannot get your own personal prayers answered with the Lord, then you will not be able to operate in the calling that God has set up for your life. This is why demons will especially target this area, so they can sever the prayer line between you and the Lord.

Your prayer line to the Lord is your lifeline. Have that lifeline damaged, cut, or severed in any way, all of the forward momentum in your calling with the Lord will completely shut down until you can get it re-established. So many believers won't pay their spiritual telephone bills (prayer, communication with God) by forgiving others, which will disconnect them from the Almighty God.

Here are some of the functioning names of the demon of unforgiveness, who will play this kind of mind game with us:

- Unforgiveness: Unwilling or unable to forgive; having or making no allowance for error or weakness. Matthew 6:12, 14–15 (KJV) reads, "And forgive us our debts, as we forgive our debtors ... For if ye forgive men their trespasses, your heavenly Father will also forgive you: But if ye forgive not men their trespasses, neither will your Father forgive your trespasses."

- Bitterness: Distasteful or distressing to the mind; exhibiting intense animosity; expressive of severe pain, grief, or regret. Ephesians 4:31 (KJV) says, "Let all bitterness, and wrath, and anger, and clamour, and evil speaking, be put away from you, with all malice."

- Jealousy: Hostile toward a rival or one believed to enjoy an advantage. Proverbs 6:34 (KJV) states, "For jealousy is the rage of a man: therefore he will not spare in the day of vengeance."
- Resentment: A feeling of indignant displeasure or persistent ill will at something regarded as a wrong, insult, or injury. Proverbs 11:29 (TLB) tells us, "The fool who provokes his family to anger and resentment will finally have nothing worthwhile left. He shall be the servant of a wiser man."
- Anger: A strong feeling of displeasure and usually of antagonism; rage. Colossians 3:8 (KJV) says, "But now ye also put off all these; anger, wrath, malice, blasphemy, filthy communication out of your mouth."
- Stubborness: Unreasonably or perversely unyielding; justifiably unyielding; suggestive or typical of a strong stubborn nature. Judges 2:19 (KJV) states, "And it came to pass, when the judge was dead, that they returned, and corrupted themselves more than their fathers, in following other gods to serve them, and to bow down unto them; they ceased not from their own doings, nor from their stubborn way."
- Envy: A feeling of resentment and jealousy toward another person because of their possessions or good qualities. James 3:16 (KJV) reads, "For where envying and strife is, there is confusion and every evil work."
- Hard-heartedness: Lacking in sympathetic understanding; a hardened heart. Hebrews 3:8 (KJV)

says, "Harden not your hearts, as in the provocation, in the day of temptation in the wilderness."

These harmful characteristics will associate themselves with the main spirit of unforgiveness. These demonic attributes will keep you from being able to forgive someone who has trespassed against you. Anger, bitterness, resentment, and a hard heart could all prevent you from being able to try to forgive someone for something bad they may have done to you in your past.

God does not want us walking around with any type of heaviness wrapped around us. And holding any type of major unforgiveness against anyone can and will be a major tool the enemy will anchor you with and wrap around your soul until you can get it completely cut away from you by the power of the Holy Ghost.

7. Sickness

As a result of the law of entropy (law of decay), when Adam disobeyed God and the fall of man was introduced to the world, Adam began the entropic degradation to the world. Because of this sin, man now will die a physical death. This is still in full operation on this earth. Every single one of us will have to battle a certain amount of sickness and illness in this life.

Oftentimes any type of sickness or illness we may get will be due to natural type causes. With all of the bad foods we eat, the pollution in our air, and normal wear and tear and aging our physical bodies will go through, all of these will contribute to our bodies breaking down with various types of illnesses and diseases at times.

However, if you study many of the deliverances that Jesus did in the gospel accounts, quite a few times a person's illness was directly due to a demonic spirit. And once that demon was cast out, then the person had a full physical healing.

These types of spirits are called spirits of infirmity, and they will specialize in attacking our physical bodies and causing them to get sick in some way. You will need proper discernment from the Holy Spirit as to whether or not someone's illness is being caused by a demon or if it is just coming from natural cause and effect from all of the different Adam-afflicted curses that are still in full play.

Here are some of the function names of the demons who will operate in this realm:

- Spirit of Infirmity. Any kind of disease or illness. Luke 13:11–13 (KJV) reads, "And, behold, there was a woman which had a spirit of infirmity eighteen years, and was bowed together, and could in no wise lift up herself. And when Jesus saw her, he called her to him, and said unto her, Woman, thou art loosed from thine infirmity. And he laid his hands on her: and immediately she was made straight, and glorified God."
- Death: The destroyer of life represented as a state of being dead. Because "all have sinned and fall short of the glory of God" (Romans 3:23 KJV), all men

are spiritually dead, separated from God who is the Source of spiritual life. Sin makes a person hate the light and despise the truth; it causes one to break God's laws and to become insensitive to holy things. Everyone who has not been redeemed by Christ is spiritually dead (Luke 15:32; Ephesians 2:1–3; Colossians 2:13 KJV).

- Anorexia: A serious disorder in eating behavior with a pathological fear of weight gain, leading to faulty eating patterns, malnutrition, and usually excessive weight loss.

- Bulimia: A serious eating disorder that occurs chiefly in females, characterized by compulsive overeating usually followed by self-induced vomiting or laxative or diuretic abuse; often accompanied by guilt and depression. 1 Corinthians 6:19 (KJV) says, "What? know ye not that your body is the temple of the Holy Ghost which is in you, which ye have of God, and ye are not your own?"

- Insomnia: An unusually abnormal inability to obtain adequate sleep. Psalm 37:7 (KJV) states, "Rest in the Lord, and wait patiently for him: fret not thyself because of him who prospereth in his way, because of the man who bringeth wicked devices to pass."

- Abnormal amounts of lethargy, sleepiness: The quality or state of being lazy, sluggish, or indifferent. Proverbs 22:13 (TLB) reads, "The lazy man is full of excuses. 'I can't go to work!' he says. 'If I go outside, I might meet a lion in the street and be killed!'"

- Epilepsy: Any of various disorders marked by abnormal electrical discharges in the brain and typically manifested by sudden brief episodes of altered or diminished consciousness, involuntary movements, or convulsions.

- Gluttony: A person who is debased and excessive in his eating habits. Gluttony is more than overeating. In its association with drunkenness (Proverbs 23:21; Deuteronomy 21:20), it describes a life given to excess. When Jesus was called a "gluttonous man," His critics were accusing Him of being loose and excessive by associating with tax collectors and sinners. Matthew 11:19 (KJV) says, "The Son of man came eating and drinking, and they say, Behold a man gluttonous, and a winebibber, a friend of publicans and sinners. But wisdom is justified of her children."

Again, you will need the power of discernment from the Holy Spirit in order to determine when you are dealing with a demon that is causing a specific type of illness or disease. But just remember, this is a type of amusement that demons can entertain themselves with by using us. Do not overlook this possibility if you are dealing with a specific type of illness or disease with someone.

Anorexia and bulimia especially should be looked at very carefully, as demons love to inflict these two if they can get away with it. If they can prevent you from properly eating, then you will not have the proper nutrients entering your body to properly function, and you could then seriously put your own life in danger if you stay in these two conditions long enough. However, gluttony will be the opposite end of this extreme. If the demons cannot try to kill you by starving your body to death, they will then try to kill you by causing you to overeat.

Many of our natural illnesses, such as heart attacks and cancers, are caused by people overeating the wrong kinds of foods over too long a period of time. And spirits of gluttony love to attach to people to see if they can get them to eat themselves to death.

8. Different Kinds of Vices

If demons will try to cause you to either overeat or undereat to try to kill you, then this next realm should come as no surprise. This is where you get into the different types of vices and addictions that are out there, and demons love to play this kind of extreme game on anyone they can.

Here are some of the main function names of these kinds of demons:

- Alcohol: ethanol, especially when considered as the intoxicating agent in fermented and distilled liquors. Proverbs 20:1 (KJV) says, "Wine is a mocker, strong drink is raging: and whosoever is deceived thereby is not wise."
- Cocaine: A bitter crystalline alkaloid obtained from coca leaves used in the form of its hydrochloride medically as a topical anesthetic and illicitly for its

euphoric effects, which may result in a compulsive psychological need.

- Heroin: A strongly physiologically addictive narcotic that is more potent than morphine and is prohibited for medical use in the United States but is used illicitly for its euphoric effects.

- Meth: An amine used medically in the form of its crystalline hydrochloride, especially in the treatment of obesity and often used illicitly as a stimulant.

- Marijuana: The dried leaves and flowering tops of the pistil late hemp plant that yield THC and are smoked in cigarettes for their intoxicating effect.

- LSD: A semi-synthetic illicit organic compound derived from ergot, which induces extreme sensory distortions, altered perceptions of reality, and intense emotional states, which may also produce delusions or paranoia and sometimes cause panic reactions in response to the effects experienced.

- Anti-prescription drugs: Titus 2:2,6 (KJV) says, "That the aged men be sober, grave, temperate, sound in faith, in charity, in patience ... Young men likewise exhort to be sober minded."

All of these vices can become extreme addictions and all shorten our life span; not to mention they can all seriously cripple us and prevent us from being able to properly function in this life and our specific callings for the Lord. Get hooked on any of these types of heavier drugs or get to the point where you have become an alcoholic, and God will then not be able to use you in the calling He has set up for your life until you can get yourself properly cleaned up and fully delivered.

Again, this is why demons will play this kind of heavy, extreme game with some of us, as they know once they can get a person hooked on these kinds of addictive substances, they will then knock that person right out of their divine destinies with the Lord. How many potential great men and women of God have never made it to the starting line with the Lord because they could never fully break free from their specific addictions?

Once demons see someone starting to dabble and experiment with these substances, they will waste no time in trying to move in for the kill, as they know they will have the appropriate legal rights to be able to attach to that person.

This is why experimenting or dabbling with some of the heavier drugs could get you into major trouble in the spiritual realm, as demons just watch and wait for people to punch a hole in their protective hedges by experimenting with these kinds of forbidden substances.

9. False Religions

Our Bible is very clear on this next issue: there is only one name and one way into heaven, directly through Jesus Christ and His sacrificial death on the cross. There are no other ways, no other names, and no other religions in this world that can get us into heaven. Jesus has made it very clear that He, and only He, is the only way into heaven and that no one will come to His Father unless they come directly through Him.

With Jesus being the only way into heaven, then it can only be expected that demons will try to conjure up as many other ways as they possibly can so they can keep people from finding the only one true Way. Hence you have many false religious systems that are still in operation in the world today.

We believe that demons are running all of these other false religious systems in the world today, and each one of these areas is a major stronghold area, with some of Satan's best and smartest demons running all of these false religious systems.

Here are the major false religious systems still in operation in the world today, with each one of them being run by demonic spirits who specialize in social and religious deception.

- Islam: The proper name of the religion known as Mohammedanism. It designates complete and entire submission of body and soul to God, his will and his service, and all those articles of faith commands and ordinances revealed to and ordained by Mohammed, his prophet. Islam, the Mohammedans say, was once the religion of all men, but wickedness and idolatry came into the world either after the murder of Abel, at the time that resulted in the flood, or only after Amru Ibn-Lohai, one of the first and greatest Arabian idolaters. Every child, they believe, is born in Islam, or the true faith, and would continue faithful to the end, were it not influenced by the wickedness of its parents "who misguide it early, and lead it astray to Magismi."

- Jehovah's Witnesses: A restoration Christian denomination with non-Trinitarian beliefs distinct from mainstream Christianity. The organization reports worldwide membership of over 7.65 million adherents involved in evangelism, convention attendance of over 12 million, and annual Memorial attendance of over 19.3 million. They are directed by the Governing Body of Jehovah's Witnesses, a group of elders in Brooklyn, New York, that establishes all doctrines. Jehovah's Witnesses' beliefs are based on their interpretations of the Bible, and they prefer to use their own translation, the New World Translation of the Holy Scriptures. They believe that the destruction of the present world system at Armageddon is imminent and that the establishment of God's kingdom on earth is the only solution for all problems faced by humankind. The group emerged from the Bible Student movement, founded in the late 1870s by Charles Taze Russell with the formation of Zion's Watch Tower Tract Society, with significant organizational and doctrinal changes under the leadership of Joseph Franklin Rutherford. The name Jehovah's Witnesses, based on Isaiah 43:10–12, was adopted in 1931 to distinguish themselves from other Bible Student groups and symbolize a break with the legacy of Russell's traditions. Jehovah's Witnesses are best known for their door-to-door preaching, distributing literature such as *The Watchtower and Awake!*, and refusing military service and blood transfusions. They consider use of the name Jehovah vital for proper worship. They reject Trinitarianism, inherent immortality of the soul, and hellfire, which they consider to be unscriptural doctrines. They do not observe Christmas, Easter, birthdays, or other holidays and customs they consider to have pagan origins incompatible with Christianity. Adherents commonly refer to their body of beliefs as "the truth" and consider themselves to be "in the truth." Jehovah's Witnesses consider secular society to be morally corrupt and under the influence of Satan and limit their social interaction with non-Witnesses.

- Mormonism: A new religion founded in the nineteenth century by Joseph Smith. The Church of Christ, which became The Church of Jesus Christ of Latter-day Saints, or Mormonism, was established on April 6, 1830, at Fayette, in the "burned-over district" of upstate New York by Joseph Smith following the publication of The Book of Mormon on March 26, 1830. Smith claimed to have derived the book from golden plates that he had discovered with the aid of the angel Moroni. He maintained that the plates were written in "Reformed Egyptian," which he had translated with the aid of the "Urim" and "Thummim," two stones through which he viewed the writings. Proclaiming himself a prophet, Smith gathered about him a following of devoted disciples. In 1840, the Mormon apostle, Orson Pratt, published an account of an encounter between Smith, God the Father, and Jesus Christ, said to have taken place as early as 1820. Today the story of this "first vision" has become one the basic apologetic claims of Mormonism, although it rests on contradictory historical evidence.

- Hinduism: The predominant religion of India. Hinduism includes Shaivism, Vaishnavism, and rauta, among numerous other traditions. It also includes historical groups, for example, the Kapalikas. Among other practices and philosophies, Hinduism includes a wide spectrum of laws and prescriptions of daily morality based on the notion of karma, dharma, and societal norms. Hinduism is a conglomeration of distinct intellectual or philosophical points of view rather than a rigid common set of beliefs.

- Buddhism: The prevailing form of religion in Eastern Asia. Buddha, the "sage," the "enlightened" (from the Sanskrit *buddh*, to know), is the title of honor given to the hermit Gotama (Gautama) or Sakyamuni (the "hermit of Sakya"), the founder of Buddhism. Buddhism rejected Brahma as the ruling spirit of the world and admits no Almighty creator. "It admits no beings with greater supernatural power than man can reach by virtue and knowledge; in fact, several of the Buddhist nations have no word in their languages to express the idea of God." Buddha takes the place of

God, for all practical purposes, in the worship and life of the people.

- Confucianism: Of or relating to the Chinese philosopher Confucius or his teachings or followers. Confucius, a Chinese reformer and moralist, was born about 551 B.C. at the village of Tseu-se in the small kingdom of Lu (now a part of the province of Shantung) and died B.C. 479. He is said to have been a descendant of the emperor Hoang-ti, who reigned B.C. 2600. When he was three years old, his father died, but his mother trained him with great care and was rewarded by the rapid progress and filial tenderness of her son. At seventeen, he was called to public life as inspector of the grain markets. He was married at nineteen but, according to some accounts, subsequently divorced his wife (after she had borne him a son) in order to devote himself to the study of the ancient writings and prepare for the work of restoring the usages and doctrines of the old sages. Confucius was a teacher of morals but not the founder of a religion. His doctrines constitute rather a system of philosophy in the department of morals and politics than any particular religious faith. Other writers have broadly asserted that he did not recognize the existence of a God
- Shintoism: "The Religion of the Kami," the term for the religion of the ancient Japanese that existed before the introduction of Confucian ethics or Buddhism into Japan and was practiced in a more or less pure form

until the restoration of the mikado to supreme power in 1868, when the government ordered a thorough purification and propagation of the ancient cult.

- Sikhism: Originally a religious sect that has since grown into a nation and inhabited the Punjab. Their founder was Nanok (q.v.), who has been succeeded by nine pontiffs, each of whom, like himself, is popularly denominated guru, or teacher. His object was to unite Hindus and Mohammedans on the basis of a pure monotheism and of human brotherhood.

- Jainism: The name of a very powerful heterodox sect of Hindus particularly flourishing in the southern and western parts of Hindustan. Their name, Jainas, signifies followers of Jina, the generic name of deified saints, but as these saints are also called Arhat, the sect is frequently called Arhatas. The tenets of this sect are in several respects analogous to those of the Buddhists.

- Zoroastrianism: A Persian religion founded in the sixth-century B.C. by the prophet Zoroaster. More correctly, Zarathustra, which in Greek and Latin was corrupted into Zarastrades and Zoroastres, while the Persians and Parsees changed it into Zerdusht, was the founder of the Parsee religion. The original meaning of the word was probably that of "chief," "senior," "high priest," and it was a common designation of a spiritual guide and head of a district or province. Indeed, the founder of Zoroastrianism is hardly ever mentioned without his family name, Spitima. He was a native of Bactria. He applied to himself the terms Manthran (reciter of "Manthras"), a messenger sent by Ahura-Mazda, or a speaker, one who listens to the voice of oracles given by the spirit of nature, one who receives sacred words from Ahura-Mazda through the flames.

- Spiritualism: A word now generally used to designate the belief of those who regard certain mental and physical phenomena as the result of the action of spirits through sensitive organizations known as mediums. Spiritualists claim that Spiritualism is but another term for the belief in the supernatural, that it has pervaded all ages and nations and that American Spiritualism is but the last blossom of a very ancient tree.

- Christian Science: A system of religious thought and practice derived from the writings of Mary Baker Eddy and the Bible. It is practiced by members of the Church of Christ, Scientist, as well as some others who are nonmembers. Its central texts are the Bible and the Christian Science textbook, *Science & Health With Key to the Scriptures* by Mary Baker Eddy. In the textbook, she describes the teachings and healings of Jesus as a complete and coherent science that was demonstrated and proven through his healings.

- Hare Krishna: The eighth and most celebrated of the ten chief incarnations of the god Vishnu, who, together with Brahma and Siva, constituted the divine triad of the Hindu mythology.

- Scientology: A body of beliefs and related practices created by L. Ron Hubbard (1911–1986), starting in 1952 as a successor to his earlier self-help system, Dianetics. Hubbard characterized Scientology as a religion and in 1953 incorporated the Church of Scientology in Camden, New Jersey. Scientology teaches that people are immortal beings who have forgotten their true nature. Its method of spiritual rehabilitation is a type of counselling known as auditing, in which practitioners aim to consciously re-experience painful or traumatic events in their past in order to free themselves of their limiting effects.

- Kabbalah: The title of the celebrated system of religious philosophy, or, more properly, theosophy, which has played so important a part in the theological and exegetical literature of both Jews and Christians ever since the Middle Ages. The doctrine was received by oral tradition. The term is thus in itself nearly equivalent to "transmission."

- Unification Church: The Holy Spirit Association for the Unification of World Christianity. Also known as the Unification Church, it is a new religious movement founded in South Korea in 1954 by Sun Myung Moon. Over the next few decades, it expanded to most nations of the world and now has five to seven million members. Unification Church beliefs are based on the Bible and explained in the church's textbook, *Divine Principle*. The Blessing ceremony of the Unification Church, a wedding or marriage rededication ceremony, is a church practice that has attracted wide public attention. The Unification Church has tried to engage in interfaith activities with other religions, including mainstream Christianity and Islam, despite theological differences. The Unification Church sponsored many organizations and projects over the years, including businesses, news media, projects in education and the arts, and political and social activism. It has a megachurch in Seoul, Korea, and the Peace Island in Liberia with the New Hope Academy situated there. The church has been led by Moon and his wife, Hak Ja Han, and in recent years also by their children.

- Freemasonry: A fraternal organization that arose from obscure origins in the late sixteenth to early seventeenth century. Freemasonry now exists in various forms all over the world, with a membership estimated at around six million, including approximately 150,000 under the jurisdictions of the Grand Lodge of Scotland and Grand Lodge of Ireland, over a quarter of a million under the jurisdiction of the United Grand Lodge of England, and just under two million in the United States. The fraternity is administratively organized into independent grand lodges or sometimes Orients, each of which governs its own jurisdiction, which consists of subordinate (or constituent) lodges. The various grand lodges recognize each other or not based upon adherence to landmarks. (A grand lodge will usually deem other grand lodges who share common landmarks to be regular and those that do not to be "irregular" or "clandestine.") There are also appendant bodies, organizations related to the main branch of Freemasonry, but with their own independent administration.

- The Children of God: May refer to People of God, a religious concept; divine filiation, the Christian concept of becoming a child of God; or an English translation of the Hindi word *harijan*, a term Mohandas Gandhi used for dalits. The Family International, founded in 1968 as the Children of God, is a religious movement. It could also refer to *Children of God*, the 1987 album by the American post-punk band Swans; *Children of God*, a 1998 science-fiction novel by Mary Doria Russell; or *Children of God*, a 2010 film directed and written by Kareem Mortimer. It is the former name of the religious sect now known as Family International. It also refers to the followers of Mary Ann Girling, also known as Walworth Jumpers.
- Eckanar: A new religious movement founded in the United States in 1965. It focuses on spiritual exercises claimed to enable practitioners to experience what its followers call "the Light and Sound of God." The personal experience of this spiritual light and sound is a primary goal of the teaching. It claims to provide a personal, unique, and individual spiritual inner path to an understanding of self as soul and development of higher awareness "consciousness" and God. According to the Eckankar glossary, the term Eckankar means

"Co-Worker with God." "Eckankar" derives from Ekank r or Ik Oank r (Sanskrit Eka Omk ra), a name for God given by Guru N nak and the very first word of the M l Mantra (recited every day by Sikhs), the Japj Sahib, and the Sri Guru Granth Sahib (Sikh holy scriptures). Since 1985, followers of Eckankar have described it as "The Religion of the Light and Sound of God." Prior to 1985, Eckankar was known as "The Ancient Science of Soul Travel," "The Science of Total Awareness," and "A Way of Life." ECK is another word for the Holy Spirit, also known as the Audible Life Current, Life Force, or Light and Sound of God. Eckankar's headquarters are in Chanhassen, Minnesota, southwest of Minneapolis. The Eckankar Temple, an outdoor chapel, an administrative building, and the ECK Spiritual Campus are located at this site.

- The Way International: A non-Trinitarian, nondenominational Christian ministry based in New Knoxville, Ohio, with home fellowships located in the United States and more than thirty other countries. It was founded by Victor Paul Wierwille in 1942 as a radio program and became The Chimes Hour Youth Caravan in 1947 and The Way, Inc., in 1955. The ministry distributes works such as *The Way* magazine through its publishing company, the American Christian Press, and has developed classes and other programs in several languages. It formed The Way Corps in 1970, a leadership training program, which continues today. The Way actively offers classes in biblical studies to its followers, highlighting The Way of Abundance and Power class series. The Way promotes itself as a biblical research, teaching, and fellowship ministry, providing service and direction on how to understand the Bible so people can apply it and manifest the more abundant life. The Way has received criticism for some of its internal policies, including a practice known as "Mark and Avoid," which instructs followers to avoid individuals whose practices cause division and offenses to the doctrine (Romans 16:17) and for its belief and promotion of living debt-free. Due to these and other practices, the ministry came under scrutiny as an alleged cult. In 2000, the president of The Way, Craig Martindale, resigned following allegations of sexual misconduct. Rosalie F. Rivenbark now heads the organization, along with four other members on the board of directors.

- Theosophy: The name given to a so-called sacred science, which holds a place distinct as well from that of philosophy as from that of theology, even in questions where these latter sciences have the same object with it; namely, the nature and attributes of God. Another name for theosophy is mysticism.

- Rosicrucianism: A pretend fraternity in Germany that existed simply in a book entitled *Fama Fraternitas des loblichen Ordens des Rosenkreuzes*, published in 1614. That book recited that Christian Rosenkreuz, a German of noble family born in 1388 and educated in a convent, had in early youth visited the holy sepulchers and spent three years in Damascus with the Arabians. He engaged in the study of physics and mathematics. After which, he went to Fez by way of Egypt and there pursued the study of magic. He learned among other things that every man is a microcosm. An attempt to dispense his newfound wisdom in Spain met with no encouragement.

- Atheism: From the Greek word (without God). In popular language, it means the negation of the existence of God.
- Legalism: In Christian theology, usually a pejorative term referring to an overemphasis on discipline of conduct, or legal ideas, usually implying an allegation of misguided rigor, pride, superficiality, the neglect of mercy, and ignorance of the grace of God or emphasizing the letter of law over the spirit. Legalism is alleged against any view that obedience to law, not faith in God's grace, is the preeminent principle of redemption.

The Weaponry of a Believer (Prayer)

2 Corinthians 10:3–5 (KJV) says, "For though we walk in the flesh, we do not war after the flesh: (For the weapons of our warfare are not carnal, but mighty through God to the pulling down of strong holds;) Casting down imaginations, and every high thing that exalteth itself against the knowledge of God, and bringing into captivity every thought to the obedience of Christ."

Prayer is one of the most misunderstood activities in the church. Prayer is more than man asking God for this or that; prayer is the kingdom concept of petitioning. Prayer is the kingdom's way of communication. Most who pray have a misconception of what prayer truly is. Prayer is not the means by which we beg for things, but on the contrary, prayer is the avenue by which we communicate with God.

In prayer, most inadvertently miss their desired target because we're either aiming in the wrong direction or using the wrong weapon. If you do not have the proper instructions on how to use a weapon, you most likely won't know which weapon to use. In turn, that weapon can and will become useless to you. Because prayer is the most important activity on earth, it actually becomes a paradox because being the most important is also the most misunderstood!

John Wesley a Methodist theologian who lived in the 1700s said, "Without GOD Man cannot, & Without Man GOD Will Not." The Bible says in John 15:5b (KJV), "For without me ye can do nothing. Which suggest to the believer that constant connection must be maintain without interruption."

There is more to understand why we as believers must stay connected if we are to achieve God's will. When we look at the scripture in Genesis, it says, "And God said, Let us make man in our image, after our likeness: and let them have dominion; over all the earth" (1:26 KJV).

The word *dominion* is very powerful because this word is interpreted as kingdom or, in other words, the king's domain. So the Word suggests that our God gave us a kingdom right here on earth, a colony, if you will, in order to broaden the kingdom of heaven. To truly understand this concept, you must look at the Bible in which manner it was written. The Bible was written with a kingdom thought.

It was written during a time when kings and queens ruled lands all over the world. Now you must understand the concept of kingdom rule. A king owns everything in his kingdom, and when I say everything, I mean everything. The king owns the forest, the trees, the squirrels, the grass, and the people; he literally owns everything in his kingdom.

If you look at history, most wars were fought over land. Kings warred over land because the more land a king possessed, the greater king he was. This concept, or should I say war, is still in play in the spiritual world.

God and Satan are at war over land. You might ask yourself, "What land is God at war over?" Well, in the book of Genesis, the Bible says man was created from the dust of the ground, which means we as human beings are made up from the dirt, that is, the land. So if you and I are land, we are in essence walking dirt.

The war rages over the inhabitants of this earth. Now with that understood, we must move forward to deeper understanding of this war.

In the book of Matthew, the word of God shares with us how the disciples of Christ ask Jesus to teach them one thing, prayer. Note that they witnessed Jesus do some amazing things, like turn water to wine, heal the sick, feed the multitudes, and bring the dead back to life. The disciples did not ask Jesus to teach them any of those things; the only thing they asked to be taught was how to pray.

The disciples noticed that every time Jesus came back from praying, He had some serious power to do some seriously amazing things. So in other words, what they were saying in my opinion was, "Don't teach me how to walk on water or raise the dead; teach us how to have the power to do all the things we have seen You do."

The greatest weapon a believer has is prayer! The old adage says, "Little Prayer, Little Power; Much PRAYER, much POWER, is so true. We should never take Prayer for granted."

Prayer Changes Things

Matthew 21:22 (KJV), "And all things, whatsoever ye shall ask in prayer, believing, ye shall receive."

In order to understand prayer, you must understand the kingdom. If you take the concept of prayer outside of the context of the kingdom, the result will be a religious activity. Understanding the purpose and the power of prayer means we must focus on the kingdom concept of petitioning.

The Power of the Human

The most powerful creature on earth is you, the human. How did this become like this? First of all, God only gave legal authority to humans.

You don't have a spirit! You are a spirit! "I am a spirit." Say that and remember that.

But you live in a dirt body. Your body is 100 percent dirt. When you leave your body, we dump it back into the dirt, no matter whether your dirt is dark or light black, white, yellow, or brown. Don't ever measure your work by your dirt because it is dirt!

The word *humus* is the word for dirt. Man is different. Man is the spirit being. The Hebrew word for man is *ish*. Let us create ish (humusish) or, put together like this (human), a spirit in a dirt body. So you are called a humusish man or a human! That's very important!

After God put the spirit in a dirt body, He said, "Have dominion over the earth!" The only creature that has legal rights to dominate and function on the earth is a human (a spirit in a dirt body). A human is the only creature on earth with legal authority to function and dominate the earth.

Any spirit without a dirt body is illegal on the earth! All believers must understand this statement. It is imperative to your prayer life, your connection to the kingdom. Now you know demons are illegal and they have no rights in the kingdom of heaven.

The most powerful weapon that you possess on earth is not your spirit; it is your body. Remember, you don't have a spirit. You are a spirit. Your body is what you use; it's not what or who you are.

This is why, when you lose your body, you too then become illegal, and you to have to get out of here. You must leave (death). Your body keeps you legal on earth. This is why demons are always trying to enter your body. They are trying to become legal.

Demonic possession is simply a demonic spirit trying to use your body to become legal so they can function on earth. That is why you can cast them out. It's because they have no legal authority. Because you have a body, you have legal authority.

God made Himself illegal on earth. Going back to prayer, in Genesis 1:26, God gave the human dominion over all the earth. He gave the human the authority here. And God will never go back on his word because if he did, we couldn't trust Him.

So since we as humans have the authority here on earth, God needs access granted to Him in order to come into your situation and regulate whatever is going on with you. When we pray, it's not to inform God; it is to allow Him in.

The Only Way

I know in the politically correct climate we are now all living in, the above statement is very extreme and controversial. But our Bible leaves us with no other logical explanation as to how the big picture is really set up.

The following scriptures will show you how God the Father is really driving home the point that no one is going to get to Him and where He lives unless they come through His Son and the blood that His Son has shed for all of us on the cross.

Simply put, we either come through the blood and the cross, or we do not come through at all. As such, there are no middle grounds or neutral areas for people to walk into if they do not want to accept Jesus. This is why all of the previous religious systems are called false religions because none will lead to true eternal salvation with God the Father. They are all dead ends being run by demons.

Once again, here are the most powerful verses in all of Scripture telling us that Jesus Christ is the only way to be able to receive eternal salvation with God the Father:

- "Nor is there salvation in any other, for there is no other name under heaven given among men by which we must be saved." (Acts 4:12 KJV)
- "For there is one God and one Mediator between God and men, the Man Christ Jesus, who gave Himself a ransom for all ..." (1 Timothy 2:5 KJV)
- "There is one body and one Spirit ... one Lord, one faith, one baptism, one God and Father of all, who is above all, and through all, and in you all." (Ephesians 4:4 KJV)
- Jesus said to him, "I am the way, the truth, and the life. No one comes to the Father except through Me." (John 14:6 KJV)
- "I am the door. If anyone enters by Me, he will be saved, and will go in and find pasture ... I have come that they may have life, and that they may have it more abundantly." (John 10:9 KJV)
- Jesus said to her, "I am the resurrection and the life, he who believes in Me, though he may die, he shall live. And whoever lives and believes in Me shall never die." (John 11:25 KJV)

- Then Jesus spoke to them again, saying, "I am the light of the world. He who follows Me shall not walk in darkness, but have the light of life." (John 8:12 KJV)
- And Jesus said to them, "I am the bread of life. He who comes to Me shall never hunger and he who believes in Me shall never thirst." (John 6:35 KJV)
- "I am the living bread which came down from heaven. If anyone eats of this bread, he will live forever; and the bread that I shall give is My flesh, which I shall give for the life of the world." (John 6:51 KJV)
- "… whoever believes in Him should not perish but have eternal life. For God so loved the world that He gave His only begotten Son, that whoever believes in Him should not perish but have everlasting life." (John 3:15–16 KJV)
- "He who believes in the Son has everlasting life; and he who does not believe the Son shall not see life, but the wrath of God abides on him." (John 3:36 KJV)
- "Therefore I said to you that you will die in your sins; for if you do not believe that I am He, you will die in your sins." (John 8:24 KJV)
- "Most assuredly, I say to you, he who hears My word and believes in Him who sent Me has everlasting life, and shall not come into judgment, but has passed from death to life." (John 5:24 KJV)
- "… And this is the testimony: that God has given us eternal life and this life is in His Son. He who has the Son has life; He who does not have the Son of God does not have life." (1 John 5:11 KJV)

- "And we have seen and testify that the Father has sent the Son as Savior of the world. Whoever confesses that Jesus is the Son of God, God abides in him, and he in God." (1 John 4:14 KJV)

As these passages are read, you should be able to feel the power and authority that is on each one of them and that God the Father is telling all of us, in no uncertain terms and very easy to understand language

- No one is going to be getting into heaven unless they come directly through His Son Jesus *and*
- Any other ways and names in this life are not going to be tolerated and accepted by Him.

The world may want us to have a politically correct and open-mindedness for all of these other false religions of this world, but God the Father is not going to, and as such and as His direct ambassadors on this earth, we have to tell the rest of the world what the real truth is.

Once you see what the real truth is through Jesus Christ, it is just heartbreaking to see so many people bound up and in captivity to all of these other false religious systems across the world. Millions and millions of people are being held behind enemy lines in all of these other false religions, and they have absolutely no idea and clue they are all on the wrong side of the fence.

This is one area where Satan and his demons have been very successful across much of the world. To think that there is only one way, one name, and one faith and that Satan has managed to create all of these other false religions in order to try to prevent people from finding this one true way is just heartbreaking!

Your Battle (Your Particular Fight)

Now that you have been exposed to the spiritual world and its influences, your mind should begin to take on a new view of spirituality. All that has been shared with you is for you to identify the enemy before engaging. I truly want the believer to understand that we have many enemies but we are not assigned to engage and fight them all. We have a specific assignment of engagement that we must obey or we can initiate our own destruction.

We have been taught for so many years about how to engage, fight, and, in fact, defeat the enemy. But today I want to let you know that all that teaching is not wrong, but our methods of engagement stand to be altered to a certain degree. We as believers must understand that our defense is our best offense. We have for so many years engaged an enemy that we were not to engage.

God said in James 4:7 (KJV), "Submit yourselves therefore to God. Resist the devil, and he will flee from you." God said to resist the devil and he will flee. He did not say to engage the devil. God said, "I will fight the battle." All he left for us to do is to resist the devil and he would flee from us. Hmmm, it makes you think.

Our actual engagement is in the resistance of the enemy; our resistance will force the enemy to vacate our lives for a season.

Our true engagement, the real battle we are to engage in, is our own issues. Those things we did not resist, those things that did infiltrate our hearts, or those spirits we let in and now we must get out, understand that this is the war we must fight.

Everything on the outside, God will fight. Everything on the inside, you must fight. I should not find myself engaging in battle in areas not assigned to me.

The sly, slick, wicked one (Satan), in all of his craftiness, wants me and you to fight a war in the wrong place. Fighting the wrong fight, the wrong battle, can and will lead to failure. But fighting the right fight you have been prepared for will give you success.

If Satan can get you to look on the outside of you instead of the inside, he has nothing to worry about as far as who you are fighting.

2 Chronicles 20:15 (KJV) states, "And he said, Hearken ye, all Judah, and ye inhabitants of Jerusalem, and thou king Jehoshaphat, Thus saith the Lord unto you, Be not afraid nor dismayed by reason of this great multitude; for the battle is not yours, but God's."

God may use you as a weapon (tool) for battle, but please remember you are not the one doing the fighting in the battle. It is God. As a soldier swings his sword in a battle, always know that God is swinging you in battle.

Now any fight on the outside God will fight for you. Trust in that because He said He would, but for that inner fight, God has given you and I the Holy Spirit in order to deal with those spirits that try to attach themselves to us and influence us to do demonic things.

Method of Attack

Once I locate the spirit that has infiltrated my life, it is imperative I take action immediately.

1. Identify demonic spirit.
2. Identify areas of my life it is attacking.
3. Locate all possible scriptures that pertain to this demonic spirit.
4. Set up a regimented prayer schedule three times a day.
5. Set up a weekly fast (one day, two days, and three days). This is your choice.
6. Memorize the scriptures you are using against this demonic attack.
7. Meditate on these particular scriptures day and night.

This methodology will fully engage the enemy and allow you to fight the fight you were assigned to fight.

Know this: you already have the victory, but sometimes we allow the enemy to infiltrate our lives and distract us from the truth. Engaging the enemy in this manner will put things back into perspective and give you the confidence you need as you prepare for the next battle.

Conclusion

The devil moves through our lives like a virus, trying to infect those with whom he comes in contact with, with the very thing that he himself is infected with. I refer to this syndrome as a mind virus.

There is a word I want to introduce to you, *meme*, that is, an idea, behavior, style, or usage that spreads from person to person within a culture.

All the demonic spirits and false religions we have been discussing is a means to expose you to some mind viruses that can possibly infect you or your family. Once you know what the sickness is, then and only then can you treat it. It's very hard to treat something you know nothing about, but once you identify the enemy, you can then come against it.

As you can see from this big list, some demons literally cover every type of evil we can think of, and to think that all of these evil demons were initially born and created in heaven by the Lord is simply mind-blowing, if you ask me.

The Bible tells us that a third of the angelic host ended up rebelling against God, and as a result, they are now all lost forever and will never, ever get another chance to get back into heaven. As a result, every single one of these demons has now descended into the dark side where they have now become nothing but pure evil. And the sum total of their existence is to now live and operate within their primary and function names so they can try to drag all of us down into their lower way of living and then eventually into the pit of hell itself. Maintain your prayer life and continually ask God to help us all!

What a sad and unbelievable reality! And to think that all of these fallen angels had it all at the very beginning of their existence with the Lord.

Knowing some of the basic primary and function names of these demons may help in some of the cases God may bring your way. Again, for the most part, demons will travel in groups or clusters, and when they are allowed to enter into a person's body, that whole group of demons will then usually move in all at once and set up shop. The group will have a head demon, or the chief demon, and the rest of the demons will then be the underlings under his direct control.

At certain times, the Holy Spirit can either give you a word of knowledge or some type of discernment as to what types of demons you are dealing with so you can find out what all of their legal rights may be. And then once you find out what all of the legal rights are, then you can proceed to properly break all of them before the Lord. And once all of the legal rights have been properly broken before the Lord, the demons will then have nothing else left to hold onto, and they will then be able to be cast out of the person with the appropriate command words.

The legalities that most demonic forces abide by are based

on the strengths and weaknesses of particular demons. For instance, a lying spirit will not tell the truth; nor will this demon kill. But be conscious that a murdering demon can and will most likely lie.

Knowing some of the basic function names and groupings of these demons will also help in giving us a heads up when demons do try to nip at us from time to time. Knowing what kind of evil they like to specialize in will help tip us off when it really is them attacking us.

If more people knew what the basic functions and games of these demons were, they would not so easily fall prey to some of their specific temptations like murder, suicide, and different types of addictions. Many cold-blooded murders could have easily been stopped dead right in their tracks if more people would have known they were being played by these demons who specialize in the negative feelings and emotions of hate, rage, anger, and murder.

Demons play some of these people just like a grand piano, and they then lead them right off the end of some serious life-and-death cliffs. Again, this is why every single church should have some kind of basic teaching on spiritual warfare so the flock will know how the enemy will try to operate against them.

The Bible has already told us that those who lack knowledge will perish and fall into captivity. And not having some of this basic knowledge on how demons can move and operate has caused many to have either seriously stumbled in their walks with the Lord or have knocked some of them right off the playing field of life itself with an early death and departure from this life. And this was all as a direct result of not knowing how the enemy can move and operate against them.

How many people have been led into murders, suicides, drug addictions, adultery, crime, and perverted sexual lifestyles, all as a direct result of demons playing them on the back end, giving them these unholy desires in the first place, and then prompting them to act out on it? And then most of these people were never stopping to think or analyze where these kinds of unholy desires were coming from in the first place. Again, a lot of this kind of demonic activity could have easily been stopped dead at the onset if more people knew how demons really operated behind the scenes.

So I say, "God bless you and happy hunting." I pray that this helps you focus on the real battle and we as believers stop fighting a false battle and engage the real one.

Printed in the United States
By Bookmasters